To_____

From_____

To Father, with Love

Wisdom from Guideposts

Norman Vincent Peale
Marjorie Holmes
Arthur Gordon
Will Rogers, Jr.
and others

DIMENSIONS
FOR LIVING
NASHVILLE

TO FATHER, WITH LOVE

This book is printed on recycled, acid-free paper.

Library of Congress Cataloging-in-Publication Data

To Father, with love : wisdom from Guideposts.
    p. cm.
    ISBN 0-687-00833-6 (alk. paper)
    1. Fathers—Prayer-books and devotions—English.   2. Fatherhood-Religious aspects—Christianity.   I. Guideposts Associates.
    BV4529.T68   1995
    242'.6421—dc20   94-35286
                                                   CIP

Scripture quotations unless otherwise noted are from the King James Version of the Bible.

Those noted RSV are from the Revised Standard Version of the Bible, Copyright © 1946, 1952, 1971 by the Division of Christian Education of the National Council of the Churches of Christ in the USA. Used by permission.

Those noted NIV are taken from the *Holy Bible: New International Version.* Copyright © 1973, 1978, 1984 by the International Bible Society. Used by permission of Zondervan Bible Publishers.

95 96 97 98 99 00 01 02—10 9 8 7 6 5 4 3 2 1

MANUFACTURED IN THE UNITED STATES OF AMERICA

Contents

FOREWORD

To Father, with Love: That is a good title. It conveys affection and caring, surely; but in it there also is a universal yearning, a longing, to be close, to be in communication, to be understood.

Most of the writers in this book are grown-up children speaking to or of their fathers, and they speak with a depth of emotion that leaves no doubt as to the importance of the father-child relationship. A father may have several children and varying degrees of closeness with each of them, but a child has only one father; the current that flows between them is unique, and the intensity of it plays a crucial part in the unfolding drama of childhood. That is why sons remember with such vividness the times their dads played catch with them or took them fishing, and daughters cherish memories of special closeness with their fathers long after grander occasions are forgotten. And reading about such events is a reminder to all of us to try to be better parents ourselves.

Once I heard a Sunday school teacher put a challenging question to a class of six-year-olds. "What," she asked them, "do you think God is like?" Some frowned, others looked puzzled, but one hand shot up immediately. "He's just like my dad," the child said proudly, "only more so!"

If any angels were listening, I think they must have nodded and smiled.

Arthur Gordon

GOD BLESS FATHERS
Marjorie Holmes

*M*y heart goes out to fathers, Lord. Bless them all.

Bless the young new father—grinning, awed, proud and a little scared as he feels the tightly curling fingers of his first child.

Keep him always close to that child, Lord. As loving and tender as he is now. But strong enough to meet its ever-growing demands.

And oh, help him really to enjoy it. Laugh with it, talk with it, listen to it—be its friend as well as its dad.

Bless the dad in the middle, Lord. The man who knows that raising kids isn't just circuses and ball games, but bills and braces, discipline and dissension sometimes.

Ease his aching bones, Lord, and his often aching heart.

And oh, Lord, bless the old father, too. The one looking back. The man who is no longer the mainspring of that strange, exasperating, demanding but so important institution, a family. His views don't count anymore . . . or so he thinks. He may even believe—wrongly—that he's no longer needed.

You, the Father of us all, surely know how each of these fathers feels. Comfort them, Lord, and help us, their sons and daughters, to show them that we do appreciate them. That we love them and feel very grateful that God gave us a glimpse of what he's really like—in them.

A LESSON IN LOVE
Norman Vincent Peale

*O*ne Christmas Eve when I was about ten or so, my father and I were passing Burkhart's Department Store in Cincinnati when a dirty old fellow in a tattered coat stopped me, took hold of my sleeve, and said, "Young man, give me something."

I pulled my arm away, gave the man a slight push, and walked on, nose in the air.

My father stopped short. "You shouldn't treat a man like that—Christmas Eve or any other time."

"But Dad," I said, "he's a bum."

"There is no such thing as a bum, Norman," my father said. "There may be some people who haven't made the most of their lives, but all of us are still children of God."

Then he took out his skinny old wallet—it never had much in it—and he handed me a dollar. And he said, "You catch up with that man. Tell him, 'Sir, I give you this dollar in the name of Jesus. Merry Christmas.' "

> **You'll never grow wiser nor more beautiful than when you're putting [these] three words to work. *Love one another.***

"Oh, no," I said. "I can't do that."

He said, "You do as I tell you, boy."

In those days, you really minded what your parents told you.

So I chased after the man and said, "Sir, I give you this dollar in the name of Jesus. Merry Christmas."

The old fellow was flabbergasted. He took off his beat-up old cap and bowed to me and said, "I thank you, young sir. Merry Christmas."

In that moment, his face became beautiful to me. He was no longer a bum.

Well, all this happened many years go, but I remember it vividly because my father gave me such a clear demonstration of the new commandment Jesus brought to us: "Love one another" (John 13:34). . . . You'll never grow wiser nor more beautiful than when you're putting those three words to work. *Love one another.*

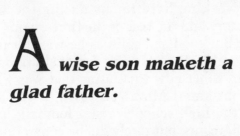

A wise son maketh a glad father.

Proverbs 10:1a

THE SIGNS OF LOVE
Dick Enberg

I always loved and admired my father. He was a good provider, working hard for us during the week in a Detroit factory and the rest of the time on our forty-acre fruit farm. But good and solid as he was, for me he had one shortcoming: He was not a demonstrative man.

I can remember how frustrating that was when I was a kid. In our small Michigan town, I was a starting player on the high school varsity football, basketball, and baseball teams, but rarely did he congratulate me on a victory or a good game. Even when I scored twenty-two points in one basketball game, all Dad said was, "How many points did the man you covered score?"

Years later, when I was living alone in California, leading the harried life of a TV sportscaster, Dad, who had been living alone on the farm back in Michigan, came to live with me. He planted fruit trees in my back-yard and cared for them like the cherry, apple, and plum

---

We know how important it is to hear our loved ones tell us that we are loved. But shouldn't we also be aware of the *unspoken* words of love? . . . Look for the signs of love.

---

trees back home. He could fix anything, and I'd tell him what a master carpenter he was. But still there was little praise from him about me and my work.

Then came his long, fatal struggle with cancer. Throughout those difficult months, I longed for an open hug from him whenever I told him I loved him, or at least a quiet, unsolicited "I love you, Son." But even on his deathbed Dad was as taciturn as always.

Later, however, I began to think about Dad and me. Maybe he had been quick to criticize and slow to compliment me, but he'd been there—for every game. And then one day, cleaning out his bedroom, I came across a half-dozen shoe boxes. Inside were hundreds of audiotapes, carefully labeled, filed, and stored. They were marked with things like "Louisville vs. UCLA Basketball, 1978," "Rams vs. Cowboys, 1973." They were tapes of the games I had broadcast, tapes Dad had secretly made by placing the microphone of his small recorder next to the radio or television speaker.

We know how important it is to hear our loved ones tell us that we are loved. But shouldn't we also be aware of the *unspoken* words of love? Those tapes told me how much my father cared. And I thought of our heavenly Father, whom we never see or touch, but the evidence of whose caring is everywhere. All those years with Dad, I just needed to look for the signs of love.

To become a father is easy, but to be a father is difficult.

American Proverb

ALWAYS KEEP TELLING ME
Jamie Buckingham

*M*y father saw old age as the greatest of all life's adventures. I loved him for that attitude, and I loved him for the venturing out in mind and spirit that he began to do as he grew older. We had always been a very "proper" family. But in his later years, Daddy finally found the freedom to put a friendly arm around a woman other than his beloved wife of more than fifty years. The older he grew, he told me, the more he realized he had confused spontaneity with impropriety. Life was too short not to show our genuine feelings.

He was not ashamed when others saw him weep when he was moved emotionally. And he loved to take my mother's hand or kiss her in front of the children and grandchildren, something we had never seen him do in his younger years. Some may have equated his "freedom" with senility or old age; I attributed it to spiritual maturity.

As I watched my father—moving rapidly toward eternity—becoming free, I realized how stiff and unyielding I remained in many areas of my life. Especially was this true in my expression of affection. Our family had never been very demonstrative. We seldom hugged and almost never kissed—at least not when I was a boy. Occasionally my mother would kiss me, but I had never, to my knowledge, kissed my daddy.

We men shook hands. Daddy taught us how to give a firm, manly handshake and how to look the other fellow straight in the eye while we were doing it. But as I watched him become free and felt my own love for him growing, I longed to express my affection in a more physical way. Yet every time I was with him and it came time to say good-bye, instead of bending and kissing him as he sat in his wheelchair, I always stuck out my hand. Even the words "I love you" stuck in my throat. I wanted to say them—but was afraid to try.

Finally, I could stand it no longer. My sophistication and my twisted concepts of masculinity were choking me. One Saturday afternoon I got in the car and made a special trip south along the Florida coast to my parents' home, thirty-five miles away. Walking into my dad's little study, I found him in his wheelchair, at work on his ledger.

"I have come for one purpose," I said. "I want to tell you something, and then I want to do something."

He looked up, grinned, and said, "Fine."

Suddenly I felt like a fool. I was forty-six years old—he was eighty-six. But I had come this far and was not going to back out.

"I love you," I said, choking up.

"Is that what you came to tell me?" he asked gently, putting his pen on the desk beside his green ledger and resting his hands in his lap.

"Yes, sir," I said.

"You didn't have to come all the way down here to tell me that," he grinned, adding, "but I'm sure glad you did."

"I've wanted to voice the words with my lips for years," I said. "I find it easy to write them on paper. And I know you have known. But it has been difficult for me to say it with my mouth. Perhaps," I added, "I needed to say it more for me than for you."

His face grew pensive, and he nodded slowly.

"There is something else," I said.

He did not look up from his place at the desk but continued to look straight ahead, nodding slowly.

I bent and kissed him, first on one cheek, then the other, then on top of his bald forehead.

He reached up, took my arms in his strong hands, and pulled me down to him so he could put his arms around my neck. For long moments we remained in that awkward position—me bending over his wheelchair, he with his arms around my neck, pulling my face up against his. Finally he released me, and I straightened up. There was a trace of tears in his eyes, and his lip quivered as he spoke.

"My father died when I was a young man back in Indiana," he said. "I left home shortly afterward to go to college, teach school and finally go to France in World War I. After the war, I moved to Florida. I never returned home except for occasional visits to see my mother.

"When my mother grew old, I invited her to come live with us." He paused, and his face broke into one of those grins. "Guess what she said? She said, 'No, I'll stay right here in Morristown in this house. But I love you for asking me to come live with you and even though I'll never do it, I hope you keep right on asking me up until the day I die.' "

Looking up at me, he added, his lip quivering again, "I know you love me. But I hope you keep right on telling me—up until the day I die."

Something broke loose in me that Saturday afternoon. Something that had been knotted up for years. Leaving my parents' house in Vero Beach, I wanted to run home, leaping and dancing, rather than getting in the car and driving back up the coast. I felt my spirit soar upward. At last I was free.

A FATHER'S PRAYER

*W*hen all is still within these walls,
And Thy sweet sleep through darkness falls
On little hearts that trust in me,
However bitter toil may be,
For length of days, O Lord! on Thee
        My spirit calls.

Their daily need by day enthralls
My hand and brain, but when night falls
And leaves the questioning spirit free
To brood upon the days to be,
For time and strength, O Lord! on Thee
        My spirit calls.

                                    Author Unknown

UNSPOKEN TREASURE
Will Rogers, Jr.

*L*ive in such a way that you would not be ashamed to sell your parrot to the town gossip," my father once said.

If Will Rogers had a rule to live by, maybe that's the one. Anyway, it's one I remember best.

Many of his words are still repeated often. However, his heritage to his children wasn't words, or possessions, but an unspoken treasure, the treasure of his example as a man and a father. More than anything I have, I'm trying to pass that on to my children.* I would like the treasure of my father's past and the best of my present to merge with their future.

The spiritual heritage we get from our parents isn't easy to pass on to our children, but I shall never cease trying.

Live in such a way that you would not be ashamed to sell your parrot to the town gossip.

---

*Written in 1957.

I remember my father with reverence and laughter. To many he was the Oklahoma cowboy, with a hair lick over his forehead, an infectious grin, twirling a long lariat, and speaking a language of his own that bit big hunks into the sham of his day. He's thought of as a humorist. He was, but he was more, too. He was never an actor, though his name blazed in lights from Hollywood and Broadway to Berlin and Alaska. He was always himself. Even as a wit he was trying to express ideas and ideals, and he would have preferred approval for them rather than applause for his humor.

I do not remember receiving very much lecturing from him at any time. He gave my sister Mary, my brother Jim, and me a good moral tone with the quiet sincerity which was always evident in all he said and did.

When I was a kid I wanted a motor to attach to my bike. I wanted it badly, maybe because none of the other kids had one. But it was very expensive, and when I asked my father for it he said no.

"But Dad, we're rich," I protested.

Well, the whole roof descended on me. He said no kid of his was ever going to parade any advantage he might have, and I'd better unlearn any such notion at once. Then he muttered something about show-offs, the poor show-off who is always lonely because he's always empty.

That made a big impression on me. Not so much the event, but the meaning my father gave it. Undue emphasis on material things made possessions ends in themselves, and that was morally wrong, if not destructive.

Growing up with that idea can make Christian ethics a habit, though at the time we didn't think of it that way, and my father didn't put it to us that way. The example is always more effective than the sermon. And he often put his ideas to us with a kind of barbed laughter. When any of us felt important or inflated with our knowledge, we had only to remember his remark: "Everybody is ignorant, only on different subjects."

> **The basic ideas of faith do not change, but how you adapt those ideas to a changing world is the important thing.**

Once, while in high school, I rushed home all excited because I'd been picked to recite a long, humorous poem. I had to try it out right away. My father retreated behind his newspaper, so I made Mother listen. Half way through I fumbled, faltered, and came to a helpless halt. Father, who I thought was paying no attention at all, came out from behind his paper and finished the whole poem. He also knew the author and when it was written. Then he went back behind his paper. I never recovered my conceit.

He was always the example. In those days, parents assumed an automatic leadership I don't see in parents today, including myself. My father was the head of the house. He behaved as the head of the house. He was the parent, kindly, generous, but definite. When he said it should be done, it was done. That fashioned us when we were young.

Sunday school for us was like going to regular school. We just went. And we were taught the reality of prayer at home. When I was about nine my father got sick. In the hushed house, my mother told us about the time all her children were sick with diphtheria. That was before I could remember. I had another brother then, Fred, who died of diphtheria; Mary and Jim and I almost did.

"But your father was down on his knees praying for all of you," Mother said. "Now let's kneel and pray for him."

We did.

He taught us to ride and rope out on a polo field near our house. I couldn't get third money in a rodeo with my rope, but I liked riding and polo, and I went to the University of Arizona so I could play it.

Well, I played it all right, and got to drinking and almost flunked out. I felt pretty miserable after that first term, and pretty ashamed. My father didn't bawl me out or cut off my allowance or anything like that. He had a better lever. It's a palpable fact that every son wants his father's respect, and at this point I wanted his desperately. His disapproving silence was like a lash. Once in a while at the table he'd mention some of the wastrels, handy examples in those days, who rode around in their cars doing nothing. The only way I could win his respect again was to switch to another university and do better.

The next term I went to Stanford and majored in philosophy. I took two courses in comparative religion, among other things, studied hard, and figured I had it all solved. One day I told my father: "That old Greek, Socrates, put it all in two simple words: 'Know thyself.'"

"Yep, and then get to know the other fellow, too," my father said. "There's always two halves to a whole."

That was pretty good for a cowboy who never got beyond the fourth grade. . . .

My father's family were Methodists and Baptists, and I remember the giggling among us kids because his sister, Aunt Sally, said it was improper to dance. Well, times change, and now most ministers think dancing is all right; and there's a lesson there:

"The basic ideas of faith do not change," my father said, "but how you adapt those ideas to a changing world is the important thing, and will determine the durability of your faith."

. . . We are given a mind by God, and that mind makes moral judgments. Only the belief that you are good, or capable of it, that your fellow man and all creatures are good, only that concept can bring you happiness. The more you practice it the better you will be.

My father lived that concept.

Will Rogers, Jr., died on July 9, 1993.

A MATTER OF CONSCIENCE
Walter "Red" Barber

I am proud that I was able to say "I love you" to two men before they died: my father, William Lanier Barber, a railroad engineer, and Branch Rickey, the legendary general manager of the Brooklyn Dodgers. They were men of strong faith; it was ever present in their daily relationships with their families, friends, and working associates.

Rickey comes vividly to mind as I am writing this on the fortieth anniversary of the season when Jackie Robinson broke the color barrier in major league baseball. Branch Rickey was directly responsible for that breakthrough. Back in those days I was broadcasting the games for the Brooklyn Dodgers, and I knew well ahead of time what Rickey was going to do. Two years earlier, in March 1945, he and I were sitting in a corner of a Brooklyn restaurant when he told me a related incident that had happened when he was a student at Ohio Wesleyan University, helping to pay his way by coaching its ball team.

> **Every night of your life**
> **when you go to bed**
> **you have to sleep with**
> **yourself.**

"One of my best players was the catcher," Rickey recalled, "a good student, the only black man on the team. When we went to South Bend to play Notre Dame, I was standing at the hotel desk as my boys each signed the register. When my catcher started to sign, the room clerk jerked the register back and snapped, 'We don't register Negroes.'

"I tried to explain, 'We're guests of Notre Dame. This is the Ohio Wesleyan University baseball team, and this is the catcher.' But the clerk wouldn't budge. So I gave the catcher my key and told him to go to my room and wait for me. When I got there I found him sitting on the edge of a chair, pulling at his hands, sobbing, 'It's my skin, Mr. Rickey, it's my skin. If I could pull it off, I'd be like everybody else.'

"The sight of that sobbing youngster tearing at his hands never left me. I decided I had to do something about it before I died."

Thirty years later Rickey was ready. And he decided that Jackie Robinson was his man for the job. Branch Rickey's family didn't want him to make the fight for Jackie Robinson. Not one person encouraged him. Some of the players threatened to resign if he signed a black ballplayer. But he persisted. And I knew why: It was a matter of conscience, the kind of courage my father inspired me with when I was growing up.

"Son," my father would say, "when you go out into the world, I can't know what you will do for a living, who you will know, where you will go. But I do know this: No matter where you go, whatever you do, who-ever you are with, *every night of your life when you go to bed you have to sleep with yourself.*"

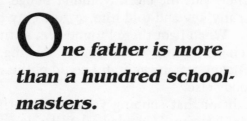

One father is more than a hundred school-masters.

English Proverb

Between Pitches
Daniel Schantz

You can have the World Series—the crowds, the instant replays, the six-million-dollar contracts, the Hall of Fame. I had something better than all of these. I had a father who played catch with me.

He wasn't much to look at, dressed in gray work slacks torn in the seat and an old dress shirt that parted at the navel where a button was missing. On his left hand he wore a plain, flat ball glove that looked like it had been run over by a truck. His smiling face was crowned with shiny black hair combed straight back.

But when my father played catch with me, he made me feel like the most important person in the world. After all, my father was a very busy man—a minister of a sizable church, among other things. Other people had to make appointments with him, but not I.

My father taught me how to throw, but sometimes I got a little too creative: fastballs, knuckleballs, screwballs. They seemed so simple for him, but at least half my attempts sailed out of control. I was always embarrassed, but he never complained. He simply trotted across the street to rescue the ball.

And when I got a pitch right down the middle, he always let me know I had done well: One side of his mouth would get a special sly grin that said "Whitey Ford couldn't have done better." I glowed at the sight of that grin, and in my mind I could hear the roar of the crowd in the stands.

31

Some days I didn't feel like setting any sports records. I just wanted to be with my dad. As the ball rhythmically glided back and forth between us, I felt very close to my father and found myself opening up to him.

"Dad, why won't Mom let us ride motorcycles?"

"Mothers have a nose for danger. Trust your mother."

"Where do people go when they die?"

"The apostle Paul says that to be absent from the body is to be at home with the Lord."

His answers were brief—telegraphed phrases that escaped between pitches. Answers that forced me to think through the questions for myself. I don't think Dad even realized he was teaching me. It was an instinct with him. Everything was an occasion to hold class. Like the way he taught me to care for my equipment:

"Here, rub some of this neat's-foot oil into your glove. It stinks a bit, but it will keep the sun from drying out the leather.

"Don't leave the ball out in the rain; it will turn hard as a rock. A new one will cost you two dollars. Money doesn't grow on trees. Take care of your equipment and it will last a long time."

I have something better than all the awards in the Baseball Hall of Fame. I have memories, memories of a father who always had time to play catch with me.

Once, when the ball hit the end of my middle finger and jammed it painfully, he taught me how to cry. With his arm around me he sympathized the tears out of me. "Doesn't feel a bit good, does it? Not a bit good." Then he taught me how to laugh. "Funny, I don't feel a thing." Then he suggested I stop crying and get on with living. "The best way to handle pain is to keep your mind busy with something else."

Now that I'm grown up I find myself practicing those side-yard lessons as if they were the Ten Commandments. When I get a little too creative as a teacher in the classroom and my methods fizzle, I remember how many times Dad chased my overthrows until I learned to control the ball. I have learned it's more important to spend time with my students, just chatting or shooting baskets, than it is to drive them to scholastic achievements that will fade with time.

I try to take good care of my equipment. My car has 120,000 miles on it, and it looks like new. Money still doesn't grow on trees.

Sometimes life hurts so bad that I just sit down and bawl. Then I make a joke and get busy.

You might think my father's side-yard coaching started me on a career in athletics, but it didn't. I flunked Little League. Too slow. Too polite. Too awkward. I don't have a single ribbon or trophy for anything I ever did in sports. But down in the basement, above my workbench, I have a rusty old can of neat's-foot oil, and every time I see it I hold it tenderly and replay in my mind the happy hours I spent with my father out on the lawn.

You see, I have something better than all the awards in the Baseball Hall of Fame. I have memories, memories of a father who always had time to play catch with me.

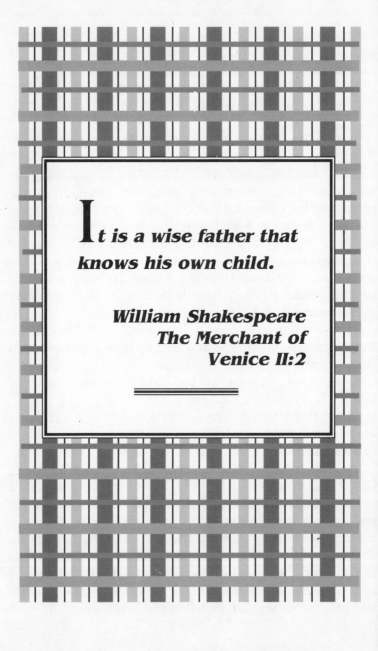

I*t is a wise father that knows his own child.*

**William Shakespeare
The Merchant of
Venice II:2**

NEVER ALONE
Reggie Jackson

*T*he letter had come to the ball park during the 1973 World Series.

It was a death threat.

As I sat in my room and again read the ominous scrawl, I shuddered. I didn't know why I got the threat.

My ball club, the Oakland Athletics, assured me there would be bodyguards. The FBI had promised they'd have people there. The whole park would be kept under strict surveillance.

Even so, what could they do for a man standing all alone out there on the diamond? I began to visualize a fanatic on a roof overlooking the park. He's holding a high-powered rifle; I'm in the batter's box waiting for the pitch. He lines up the cross hairs of the telescope sight and slowly squeezes the trigger. . . .

I jumped from the chair in my room and shook my head. *That's no way to think,* I scolded myself. Yet I wondered, *How will I feel out on that field tomorrow? Will I be so apprehensive that I can't function?* I could see myself looking over my shoulder. *What's that glint on the grandstand roof? Who's in that low-flying helicopter?*

I knew I could never play ball that way. Having a fear inside oneself is more crippling than a pulled hamstring muscle. I stepped over to the window, slumped in a chair, and picked up another letter that had come that day. I smiled as I reread it. It was from Dad back in Philadelphia.

"Dear Son," he had started, following the salutation with his usual admonitions to hang in there against left-handers, to be quick with the bat. That was Dad, always teaching.

When you lose [self-respect], other people won't respect you either.

I leaned back and shut my eyes. . . .

Crack! I'd nailed one! Sent that ball right into the blue. They're screaming. I run, but it's only fifteen feet to first base. The base is a garbage-can lid next to the old board fence. And we're having the game of the year in our back yard in Wyncote, Pennsylvania.

The screen door creaks and Dad steps out. He's been pressing pants since seven this morning. It's steaming inside his little tailor shop. Now he stands blinking and smiling in the sun, wiping the sweat from his creased forehead and settling down for a moment with an appraising eye to watch us play.

Every so often he'll advise. "Now, Reggie, you just put that shoulder into it more." Or, "Jim, you're standing too far back from the plate."

We listened. Dad had played semipro ball. I thought he was as good as DiMaggio and Rizzuto put together. But back then his color had kept him out of the majors.

Dad taught us things other than how to swing a bat. One day when I was eight I was helping him make deliveries. He'd pulled the old panel truck up to a grocery store and I went in to buy some bread and milk.

When I came out I also carried a candy bar. Shoplifting was an everyday sport with us neighborhood kids.

Dad's big hand gripped my arm.

"Where'd you get that candy bar?"

"Found it."

"Like nothing you found it! You take that bar back to the cashier and tell her you took it."

I stared at him, wide-eyed.

Going back into that store was the last thing I wanted to do. But the look in Dad's eye assured me there could be something worse.

After I came back, Dad didn't start up the truck. Instead he turned to me. "Look here, son," he said, his hand on my shoulder. "Don't you know the difference between right and wrong? It's bad enough when you take what doesn't belong to you from others, but what's worse is what it does to you. You're hurting yourself," he emphasized, pointing to his heart, "right here. It's costing you your own self-respect. And when you lose that, other people won't respect you either."

There were many similar talks that followed. Dad called God, The Man Upstairs. "He knows what you're doing all the time, son," he said. "Play square with your fellow man—no lying, no cheating or stealing—and The Man Upstairs will take care of you."

Dad's simple theology became the basis of my faith.

Not only did I never steal again, but I learned to respond to that inner voice that told me whether I was doing right or wrong.

Dad said Jesus was sent by God to show us how he wants us to live. "Sure," Dad said, "we can't always do right—I sure do make my own mistakes—but it's important that we *try* to do what he wants. And remember," he added, "it isn't enough just to believe in God. You've got to *know* him."

From Dad's teachings I gained a deep inner peace, a sense of protection, an assurance that all would be well if I tried to play square with the other guy, that God would take care of me. . . .

Thinking back to my father's assurance that The Man Upstairs would take care of me, I was suddenly able to shrug off the death threat and I was filled then with a renewed sense of that deep inner peace.

It isn't enough just to believe in God. You've got to *know* him.

Eighteen hours later I was in the batter's box facing a fireball man on the mound. The crowd was going wild. But I had my mind only on that ball. I wanted a fast one so I moved up in the batter's box as though I was expecting a curve. He tried to blow one by me. I was ready. *Whupp! Sock!*

I was rounding third base when the realization struck me. I had forgotten all about the death threat. I knew Dad was watching our game on television back in Philadelphia and that he must have heard about the threat against my life. I looked up where the TV cameras were and waved. I know he got the message.

H
onour thy father and thy mother: that thy days may be long upon the land which the Lord thy God giveth thee.

Exodus 20:12

THE GREATEST GIFT A FATHER CAN GIVE

Justin Fisher

I had always felt that my father was a religious man. He went to church each Sunday, sang every hymn, and was a good example of a truly successful man. But until two tragic incidents came into my father's life several winters ago, I had never fully understood what it is to be a truly religious man. The faith he gave me was the greatest gift a father can give a son.

One school night as I studied my chemistry, I heard the fire alarm blow loudly. In a rural community like ours there is only a volunteer fire department. I hurried outside to join the others who were watching the firemen rush to the blaze. As I glanced upward, I realized that the billows of smoke filling the darkening night were coming from the direction of my father's furniture store.

Minutes later I stood beside my parents and watched one of Indiana's most fashionable furniture stores go up in flames. As hundreds of community residents rushed to save the furniture from the fire, I studied my parents' faces carefully. The yellowish light from the blaze reflected the grief in their faces. They did not shed a tear; they looked straight ahead and held their heads high.

Later that evening we returned home. The damage already had been estimated at $250,000, and the fire was still blazing. We gathered in the den and quietly thought about the evening. Finally Father spoke. I had expected him to just give up. He and his brother had worked for eighteen years to build an ideal furniture outlet, one that was awarded a national prize. Now that proud store was a pile of black ashes.

To my surprise, Father gave thanks to God in those quiet moments. He thanked God for a wonderful family, many wonderful friends, and above all, an undying faith. I couldn't believe my ears! How could he be so thankful? How could God do such a thing to us? How would we survive?

> **True faith never hides behind weak people. It is a prized possession that must be cleaned and polished regularly.**

I didn't sleep well that night. I kept thinking about my father. His whole life had been destroyed, and yet he was willing to strike out again, to rebuild his loss because of a faith! Where was mine?

The very next day Father began rebuilding his dream. Along with his brother he worked long and hard each day, and there were many problems.

Finally the store was reopened, more beautiful than before, all because Father never gave up.

And then the second tragedy struck. We found out Father had active tuberculosis. He was immediately put to bed, isolated, and confined to his room for a period of six to eight months. I was stunned. For a while, I hated God. Then I began to notice Father. He never blinked an eye when told of his illness. He went to bed, and I heard him remark again how thankful he was that he had a faith to live by.

I learned a great deal that summer by watching over Father. He didn't complain once. He learned Spanish as a hobby and never let us become discouraged, even when things seemed as if they could never be made right again. As I tried to make him happy and comfortable, I began to look at myself. Could I ever have as much faith as he had? How could I develop it?

As I tried to help him, I found myself being helped. Each day a little of his belief began to take root in me. I began to realize that true faith never hides behind weak people. It is a prized possession that must be cleaned and polished regularly. It is a smile on a sick person's face, a kind word to a forgotten soul, an unfailing witness to a changing world. Faith, I discovered, is life itself.

Father is much better now. The doctors are amazed at his progress, and we are all awaiting the day when he can return to a normal life. He is, for me, a truly great man, and even though his tragedies have been crushing ones, the faith of each one of us has been strengthened greatly through these past months.

I have always felt that my father was a religious man. Now I know it for a fact. The faith he has shown to me will always be my most prized possession.

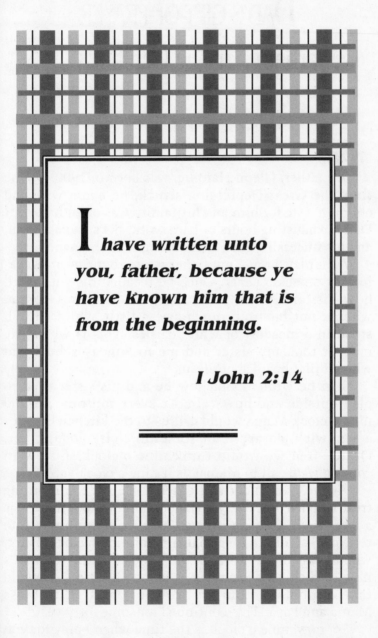

I have written unto
you, father, because ye
have known him that is
from the beginning.

I John 2:14

DAD'S GIFT OF PRAYER
Barbara Harding Oehlbeck

*M*y father, Glenn Harding, was born in 1900. By the time the Great Depression struck, he had a wife and children. Life for him and his family was often hard, but Dad's exhausting hours of hard work, his steadfast faith, and his unceasing good cheer brought us through.

When I left home, my father wrote to me every week, mostly on scrap paper. Once he recalled his youth and how his family had moved from Indiana to Georgia, where "not far from our house a little white church stood in a meadow of white daisies. This is where my mother took my sister and me to Sunday school and where I first heard about Jesus."

Then he wrote about how he and his sister used to play outside and how "almost every morning around nine o'clock Mama would call us to the kitchen door for a sandwich, an apple, or something else good to eat. Quite often we would think nine o'clock so slow in coming we'd call to Mama, 'Is it nine o'clock yet?'

"As we grew older and entered school, the morning treat stopped, but every afternoon after school there was a sandwich waiting for us. And when summertime returned, so did that special time of nine o'clock. Later, when I was on my own, I could not forget my mother's nine o'clock call. Each day at about that time, I would take a moment from my work to ask God to bless Mama and Papa. This continued for some forty years.

"So, now, nine o'clock is the time when I pray for you

children. I envision Jesus at Robert's farmhouse as the family there goes about its chores, and with Buddy as he teaches his students. He is with Vivian, and her husband, Jack, as he leaves for work on the railroad. He's with Iva and her family in their new home. And he's with you too, Barbara, as you sit watching the sunrise you often write to me about."

Nowadays my father lives in Virginia and my husband and I live in south Florida, and on this very day I am about to write him another letter. But I must stop. It is nine o'clock. Time to say a prayer.

WHEN FATHER PRAYS

When father prays the house is still,
his voice is slow and deep.
We shut our eyes, the clock ticks loud;
so quiet we must keep.

Sometimes the prayer gets very long
and hard to understand,
and then I wiggle up quite close,
and let him hold my hand.

I can't remember all of it,
I'm little yet, you see;
but one thing I cannot forget,
my father prays for me.

Author Unknown

A GOOD LISTENER
Lorne Greene

*W*hen I was playing Ben Cartwright, the father in the *Bonanza* television series, I was talking one afternoon with Joe Reisman—my friend and record producer—about my own father.

Dad was a big, gentle man who had the wonderful gift of being a good listener. I was telling Joe all about this—especially about the time that gift of his helped me make a crucial decision.

I had enrolled in the chemical engineering course at Queen's University in Kingston, Ontario, but I had another love, too. I wanted to be an actor. As soon as I started taking classes, I discovered that only people in non-lab courses could go out for the Drama Guild. Suddenly I wanted to talk this over with Dad. I called him on a pay phone and raced the three-minute limit to get it all said.

"Isn't this a coincidence!" Dad interrupted me. "I'll be passing through Kingston tomorrow on my way to Toronto. Why don't I stop by the school and you can tell me more?"

> **One of the most powerful insights a father can give his children about God [is] *You can talk to the Man.***

The next afternoon I poured out my thoughts and dreams for the future, and by the time I finished I had chosen my career—in the theater.

I explained to Joe what I later found out. "My dad didn't have to go to Toronto at all. He made that hundred-mile trip because he knew I needed him to listen. You know, Joe," I added, "I could always talk to the man."

As a record producer, Joe had a sharp ear for new material, and he jotted down some of the things I'd said about my father. Eventually his notes found their way to Merle Kilgore, a songwriter. Here's what Merle did with them:

Yes, you can talk to the Man;
He's got time; He'll understand;
He's got shoulders big enough to cry on.
Tell all your troubles, take your time;
He's in no hurry; He doesn't mind.
It matters not how bad you've been,
You can talk to the Man.

Now I'd been talking about Dad. But by the time Merle set the words to music and we'd made a record of them, "Man" had become capitalized, and the record was about God, the Father of us all.

That's a natural progression, when you think about it, because we depend on the same accessibility, the loving attention of a father on earth, when we pray to our Father in heaven.

To me, it's one of the most powerful insights a father can give his children about God: *You can talk to the Man.*

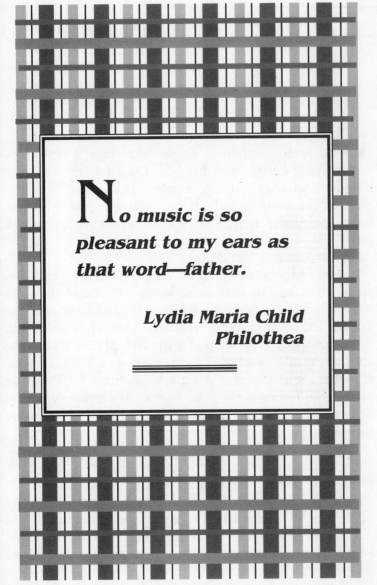

No music is so pleasant to my ears as that word—father.

Lydia Maria Child
Philothea

THE NIGHT THE STARS FELL

Arthur Gordon

One summer night in a seaside cottage, a small boy felt himself lifted from his bed. Dazed with sleep, he heard his mother murmur some protest about the lateness of the hour, heard his father laugh. Then he was borne, with the swiftness of a dream, down the porch steps, through dunes humped like furry camels in the darkness, out onto the beach.

Overhead, the sky blazed with stars. "Watch!" his father said, and incredibly, as he spoke, one of the stars moved. In a streak of golden fire, it flashed across the astonished heavens. And before the wonder of this could fade, another star leaped from its place, and then another, plunging toward the restless sea. "What is it?" the child whispered. "What's happening?" "Shooting stars," his father said. "They come like this every year on certain nights in August. I thought you'd like to see the show."

That was all: just an unexpected glimpse of something haunting and mysterious and beautiful. But back in his bed, the child stared for a long time into the dark, rapt with the knowledge that all around the house the night was full of the silent music of the falling stars.

Decades have passed since then, but I remember it still because I was the fortunate seven-year-old whose father believed that a new experience was more important for a small boy than an unbroken night's sleep. No doubt in my childhood I had the usual quota of playthings, but these are forgotten now. What I remember is the night the stars fell, and the day we hitched a ride in a caboose, and the time we tried to skin the alligator, and the telegraph we made that really worked. I remember the "trophy table" in the hall where we children were encouraged to exhibit things we had found—snake-skins, seashells, flowers, arrowheads, anything unusual or beautiful. I remember the books left by my bed that pushed back my horizons and sometimes actually changed my life.

> **The easiest door to open for a child, usually, is one that leads to something you love yourself.**

My father was neither rich nor famous but he had the gift of opening doors for his children, of leading them into areas of splendid newness. This subtle art of adding dimensions to a child's small world doesn't call for money. It doesn't even require a great deal of time. It simply involves doing things more often with our children instead of for them or to them.

This is where we modern parents are falling down. We blame the pace of modern living, but we are the ones who set the pace. We deplore the availability of push-button entertainment, but we are the ones who become addicted and pass the addiction on to our children. We hire experts to coach and teach them, telling ourselves that the quality of instruction is better. Maybe it is, but it is bought with money, not given for love. And our children know the difference, even if we don't.

The generation ahead of us was wiser. Parents were not afraid to ignore their children when it suited them. But then suddenly, without warning, they would invite them to become fellow adventurers—co-conspirators, almost—in wonderful spur-of-the-moment plots designed to abolish boredom and blow away the dust of drudgeries. . . .

The easiest door to open for a child, usually, is one that leads to something you love yourself. All good teachers know this. And all good teachers know the ultimate reward: the marvelous moment when the spark you are breathing on bursts into a flame that henceforth will burn brightly on its own. Last summer, at a golf tournament, a pig-tailed ten-year-old played creditably in the junior girl's division. Even after she was eliminated, she turned up day after day to watch the other players. "How long have you been interested in golf?" someone asked her. "I got it for my ninth birthday," she said. "You mean your father gave you a set of clubs?" "No," she said patiently, "he gave me *golf*."

A whole new world, she meant, a limitless new horizon. The possessor of a wonderful realm had wanted his child to share and join him in the magic kingdom. And what a reward for both of them! And it need not have been golf. It might have been music, or astronomy, or chemistry. . . .

This is the art we parents must practice more diligently than we do. We have an eager and captive audience: children are naturally inquisitive. The chief requirement is a willingness on our part to say "Let's" more often—*let's* go, *let's* try, *let's* do—instead of "Why can't you watch television?" or simply "Run along and play."

This, surely, is the most valuable legacy we can pass

on to the next generation—not money, not possessions, not houses or heirlooms, but a capacity for wonder and gratitude, a sense of aliveness and joy. Why don't we work harder at it? Because we're human, probably. Because, as Thoreau said, our lives are frittered away in detail. Because there are times when we don't have the awareness or the selflessness or the energy.

> **This, surely, is the most valuable legacy we can pass on to the next generation . . . a capacity for wonder and gratitude, a sense of aliveness and joy.**

And yet, for those of us who have children and care what becomes of them, the challenge is always there. None of us meets the challenge fully, but the opportunities come again and again. Many years have passed since that night in my life when the stars fell, but the earth still turns, the sun still sets, night still sweeps over the changeless sea. Next year August and its shooting stars will be here again. And next year . . . next year my son will be seven.

W e never know the love of our parents for us 'til we have become parents.

Henry Ward Beecher
Proverbs from
Plymouth Pulpit

How to Raise a Lifelong Learner

Carol Gillis Zetterberg

I remember the night years ago when I was standing on a stormy ocean beach, aiming my flashlight out at an imaginary ship at sea. *Dit-dot, dot-dit*, I flashed in the darkness, in one of my father's many inspired lessons for his children. To this day I owe what I know about Morse code, ships, and the sea to my dad, George Gillis. More than that, I owe him a great love of learning.

A professional educator, Dad was always developing new ways to help children learn, but his work didn't stop at school. One of the best lessons he brought home was how a parent can be a child's best teacher. Having been a teacher myself, I'm familiar with drills, flash cards, books to read, and exercises to perform in the classroom. But Dad taught me that there is always something more that can—and should—be done by a parent at home.

1. Seize the moment.

Once while driving home on a summer night, Dad stopped the car and we hiked across a farmer's fields toward an agricultural plant, where hops were being processed. When Dad asked if we could have a tour, the foreman was too startled to refuse. As I smelled the hops, heard the whine and clatter of machinery, and saw the workers bending over miles of conveyer belts, I learned more about agricultural processing than I would ever gain from textbooks.

2. Teach by doing.

A child learns best when all the senses are involved, whether flashing Morse code or touring a hops plant. Once Dad took my Sunday school class panning for gold. We were thrilled with the shimmering dust in our pans, only to discover that it was pyrite. Besides getting a good lesson in geology, we also found that all that glitters is not gold.

3. Praise.

Whenever Dad heard me carping at my brothers or sisters, he had me say three positive things to balance out the criticism. He knew that such criticism is a source of anxiety for all children. Conversely, his favorite words for any child were "You're a champion." It's amazing that many of the kids he touched lived up to his evaluation.

4. Let your child make mistakes.

At age eight, I decided to become a chicken farmer and soon discovered that adorable young chicks become scrawny-necked tyrants who care only about being fed. I hadn't counted on the money it took to keep up with their appetites. My business venture ultimately failed, but I learned many valuable lessons (including how much work it takes to earn a quarter). Mom and Dad probably cringed watching me, but staying out of the way was the best way to help.

5. Read, read, and let them read.

Our house was filled with books, and they were all available. Even when I washed the dishes as a girl, I was allowed to prop a book up on the soap dish and read while I worked. I'm sure I could have been more efficient (and the dishes cleaner) if I hadn't read, but I treasured the ideas I discovered in those hours alone with a book and a sink full of suds.

6. Take them to church.

A study Dad conducted in one school district indicated that the children who attended church regularly tended to score higher in nationwide standardized tests. I know that growing up in a church gave me a set of values and a group of friends. I found opportunities to sing, study, and play. My friends and I developed leadership and speaking abilities. Most importantly I learned about a loving God who accepted me through all the struggles of my school days—and beyond.

THE GIFT INSIDE THE GIFT

Burl Ives

*W*henever I've had to ask myself, "What makes a gift special?" my mind goes back to one memorable night in my childhood . . . to the tenant farm my father worked in southern Illinois.

That long-ago night a sudden storm shivered the earth, a terrible assault of thunder and lightning. A shattering bolt blazed across the sky, and my father yelled, "That one hit Jim Parr's place!" Father stood six feet and weighed over 200 pounds, but he took off like a deer. Jim Parr was a neighbor, and Father believed that you do unto a neighbor what you know he would do unto you.

Father helplessly watched as the flames turned Jim's grange to ashes. He shepherded Jim, his weeping wife, and their ten children to our house. Mother built a fire to warm them and dry their clothes, their only remaining worldly goods.

> **It's the gift inside the gift that matters.**

That night we six young Ives children shared our beds with the ten young Parr children. The next day nine were taken to relatives and neighbors. Jim, his wife, and their baby stayed in our house.

Within a day or two, Father fixed a big hayrack to his wagon, hitched up a team of horses, and visited surrounding farms to collect necessities for the Parrs, unaware that two other farmers were doing the same thing.

They learned of each other's efforts at nightfall when they brought their loaded wagons to an untenanted farm, where the Parrs would start anew. Into the house went furniture and bedding, kitchenware and a stove, clothes, a ham, a can of lard. Into the barn went a hog, a horse, cow and calf, sheep, harness.

And then, finally, from Father's wagon came one last gift, a faded picture of a landscape in an old frame.

Someone sized it up and laughed. "Now what good is that old picture goin' to do the Parrs?"

My father knew where the good was. "Being old don't matter," he said. "It's the gift inside the gift that matters."

What did my father mean? That the gift he was really giving was one of good wishes, of the hope that the Parrs would again be happy—and that through this landscape the Parrs' bare house would have one touch of beauty. The gift inside the gift was loving-kindness.

And that's the gift I'm always hoping will be inside the gifts I offer.

DOING OUR BEST
Jeff Japinga

I grew up in Holland, Michigan, a small city on the shore of Lake Michigan. Holland is the home of Hope College, a school of 2,500 students. In the summer most of them went off to summer jobs or maybe to the beach. Some of the Hope staff were still on hand, though, and a lot of summers I'd help out some of them.

I remember especially one of those hot August dog days. With football practice just a week away, the time had come for Bunko to paint side- and yard lines. Bunko's real name is Norman, and he's the athletic equipment manager at Hope. That August day I was his able assistant.

Lining a football field sounds simple. You cut the grass very short where the yard lines are to go, fill up a special vacuum sprayer with white paint, and then lay down twenty-five straight lines. Easy, right? Well, not on Bunko's field. You see, every line had to be *perfectly* straight. Extra care is what he expected of me.

[His] concern was committing ourselves to doing our best, no matter what we're doing.

We stretched a four-hundred-foot string across the grass to provide a guideline for the paint machine. All that blistering afternoon, backs beginning to ache, we made sure all lines were straight and square. What seemed to make this all absurd is that in one week this field would be unceremoniously torn up by 125 pairs of football cleats. Why bother being so careful?

But that day set me straight about straight lines: Bunko's concern was committing ourselves to doing our best, no matter what we're doing. Straight lines were just one way of Bunko's proving this lesson. I've since seen the same care and diligence in the way he treats the hundreds of people he comes in contact with each week, whether its the college president or a student who needs his shoulder pads repaired. Bunko's "office" is always buzzing with laughter; people feel good there.

Ask Bunko about all this, and he'll tell you he's just an ordinary guy doing his best. And perhaps that's all it is. But I can tell you that Bunko has made life extraordinary for a lot of people—especially me—with his very ordinary creed.

Now that I'm working at Guideposts in New York City, I still try to live up to Bunko's creed. My job is finding good books for the Guideposts book programs, and when my pile of thick manuscripts seems as overwhelming as a big unlined field on a hot August day, I picture Bunko with his lining string, and then I realize that the pile deserves my best effort.

I owe Bunko a lot, so I'll make this last line about Bunko as straight as I can. Thanks, Dad.

And, ye fathers, provoke not your children to wrath: but bring them up in the nurture and admonition of the Lord.

Ephesians 6:4

THE TEAM
Al Wall

I am in right field on a softball diamond. I am not here because I want to be. I am here because I am the coach and we are a man short. If I didn't play, we would have to forfeit a crucial game.

There are several reasons I would rather not be here. I am forty-seven years old. The next oldest man on the field is, maybe, twenty-five. Softball is misnamed. There is nothing soft about a line drive from a few yards away, or the blur of a fastball coming at you from that oh-so-close pitcher's mound.

The first inning is dragging. The pitcher is taking his time, and he has a fastball that causes an endless number of foul tips. But I'm happy out here. I've always loved the ball field.

Growing up in the North Carolina foothills, I played fast-pitch softball whenever I could. At the tender age of seventeen I managed a furniture manufacturer's entry in an industrial league. Later I played for and coached two city-league championship teams. My wife, Helen, even let me name our only son for the man I most respected in baseball, Stan Musial of the St. Louis Cardinals.

I wanted young Stan to play ball, too. I dreamed of the day when we might even play together, but there was that afternoon when Stan was one year old, and he fell on an in-floor furnace grill and burned both hands severely. Oh, the fear I felt for him. That night I prayed as I never had before. . . .

A lanky center fielder comes toward me. "Coach," he says apologetically, "I guess your arm isn't what it used to be, so if we ever get anything out here that's coming your way, flip the ball to me and I'll play toward right center on left-handed batters."

His offer is not only deeply appreciated, it is prophetic.

The very next pitch results in a liner coming straight at me. Instinctively, I go down on one knee to block the ball. I field it and in the same motion toss it to the center fielder, whose relay throw holds the base runner to a single. The inning ends with a double play.

As we head for the dugout, the lanky center fielder comes over to me and says, "Well, Coach, we made that one work, didn't we?"

I reply, "Yes, Stan, we sure did."

I look again at my son, whose hand rests on my shoulder as we leave the field. As we reach the bench, a thought races through my mind: It isn't Busch Stadium, it's Orange Grove Park. It isn't the St. Louis Cardinals, it's Fort Johnson Baptist Church. It isn't the big league, but it's the best league—-where father and son make a team.

A CHEERFUL LOSER
Toby Smith

Sometimes when I hear of parents mercilessly pushing their children to excel at everything, I think of my own father and what his attitude was.

Though he greatly enjoyed sports, Dad was not an athlete by any means. He liked golf, but to my knowledge he never broke 100. He loved football, but he never once threw me a spiral. He liked swimming too, but he never set any records.

In his late thirties, Dad took up tennis. He had odd, self-taught strokes and wore baggy white shorts on the court. If he flubbed a forehand, he'd crack a joke or maybe look heavenward and laugh.

Since tennis was my passion as a boy, I couldn't understand Dad's attitude. I played only to win. If I lost, I was impossible to talk to for a week.

When I was thirteen, Dad asked me to play with him in a parent and child tournament. I hedged a bit but finally agreed.

"Only if you'll take it seriously," I said.

"Sure, sure," he said to me, smiling.

Thus an unlikely doubles team was born: a tempestuous son and his happy-go-lucky father. Somehow, we managed to win our first two matches. One more win and we'd be in the finals.

Our opponents turned out to be a girl from my junior-high class and her mother. I was mortified. Though they were only fair players, I couldn't help thinking what my school pals would say should I lose.

But what begins in fear often ends in folly. I became so frightened at the thought of being beaten that I came unglued and played horribly. My biggest concern, though, was my father.

"Dad," I kept muttering in annoyance, "you've got to try harder." I wondered why I ever let myself be talked into playing with him.

Finally, when it was over and we had lost, I didn't have the grace to shake hands with the winners. Instead, I ran off with tears in my eyes, leaving my father behind to make apologies.

Later, back home, I was still fuming when I saw Dad again. He gave me a long level stare. "You took all the fun out of it," he said quietly. "I wanted to win too, but not that badly."

Suddenly I realized Dad had tried his best—just as he did in everything else. But to him having fun was more important than coming out on top. Because I placed winning so high, I had blinded myself to all the simple joys Dad found in playing the game, benefits I'd selfishly taken away from him.

It's been said that God likes a winner, but I'm certain he likes a cheeful loser even more. I know that's how Dad would have looked at it. Over the years since that match, no matter what I've attempted, I've tried not to set my sights only on winning. That way I've found that—win or lose—you can still experience the wonderful delight of just doing.

> **It's been said that God likes a winner, but I'm certain he likes a cheerful loser even more.**

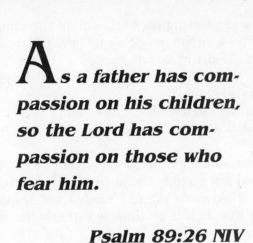

As a father has compassion on his children, so the Lord has compassion on those who fear him.

Psalm 89:26 NIV

SOMEONE TO HOLD THE LADDER

Dan Harmon

*F*ather was painting the back wall of the sanctuary in our church—a man's work—and though I was hardly more than a fledgling youth, I asked if I could help.

He didn't say, "Thanks, but no, you might get in my way—you run along."

What Father did say was, "Sure, Son, I need your help. You stand down there and hold the ladder while I paint."

He knew, of course, that the strength in my small body would not have been much help if the ladder had slipped, but he made me feel needed and responsible. I held onto that ladder as though Father's life depended on it.

Soon he yelled down, "Hey, Son, I need a smaller brush for the trim work. How about going downstairs and getting one for me?" He may have figured I would get the wrong brush and that he might save time by getting it himself, but if he had such thoughts he left them unsaid.

Father had planted within me the seed of *needfulness*, the need for each of us to do his or her part. . . .

Later he sent me out after cleaning rags and paint solvent and other items; little errands that made a boy feel very useful and a big help to his father. Each time I returned I would manfully grasp the ladder and brace it. The thought did not occur to me that there was no one to hold the ladder while I was off getting those things Father had asked for.

Several hours later he came down the ladder, wiped his hands, and put his arm around me. We looked for a moment at the freshly painted wall, so white and glistening it seemed to light up the church.

Then he turned to me and said, "Son, I'd say *we* did a pretty good job of painting, wouldn't you?"

I beamed at him and said with a big proud grin, "Yes, sir, Dad, we sure did."

Years later, I came to realize that Father had planted within me the seed of *needfulness*, the need for each of us to do his or her part, to take an eager pride in being able to help, or to do some job that needs to be done—no matter how unimportant it may seem. And it crossed my mind that God's work is just about the same. There are so many "little" jobs that beg to be done. The offer to help out, to be part of a team, to try to do one's best, is a direct expression of the Godly spirit.

And in such a spirit one realizes that there isn't any such thing as a trivial task or an insignificant job.

Beyond the Darkness
Raymond W. O. Knowles

*W*hen I was a boy on a farm, my father used some of the long winter evenings to repair harness in our kitchen.

One night he asked me to go to the barn to get some whang leather and some copper rivets. I didn't want to go. He asked, "Why not?" I told him I was afraid of the dark.

My father got a kerosene lantern, lit it, handed it to me, and said, "Come on, Son."

I followed him out the back door, across the porch, and to the back steps, where he stopped. He asked me how far I could see by the lantern I was holding. I said, "I can see to the back-yard gate."

"Walk to the gate," he said. I did.

Father stayed on the back steps, and when I reached the gate, I stopped.

Father called, "Now, how far can you see?"

"I can see to the gate into the barn lot."

He called back, "Walk to it."

When I did, my father asked, "Now, how far can you see?"

"I can see the barn door." He told me to walk to the barn door.

I opened the barn door and went inside where the lantern made plenty of light. I got the whang leather and copper rivets and went out.

I could see the barnyard gate, and walked to it, then I could see the back-yard gate and walked to it.

From the back-yard gate I could see the steps to the back porch, and I walked to the steps and up onto the porch where my father was waiting. He put his arm around me, and we went into the house.

Throughout life I haven't been able to see all the way through some of the experiences that have come to me. But as I have tried to carry the "light" which is Jesus Christ into every experience, I always have found that he gives enough light to show me the next step. I can find my way to where he wants me to go.

If I could see all the way, then I would trust only myself, but being able to see only step by step, I have to trust him. And he has never failed me.

WHEN YOU CAN'T SMILE
Tommy Lasorda

*T*ime and again while I was growing up I'd hear my father say, "If you can't smile, borrow someone else's."

He practiced what he preached, too. He used to sit at the head of the dinner table with a big grin on his face and say, "I'm the luckiest man in the world."

One day I said to him, "Pop, how can you say that? You work in a stone quarry driving a truck, and in the winter you come home so cold that we have to take your shoes off and massage your feet to get them warm again. Mom has been sick and has arthritis so bad she goes to the doctor. You have five sons you have to feed and clothe. And every paycheck you get on Friday belongs to someone else. How can you say you're the luckiest man in the world?"

He looked at me and said, "You want to know why? Because when I came from the old country to this great country, I had nothing. Now I got a wonderful wife and five wonderful sons. I got a little house that I worked hard for, and I got an old car out front that I can drive. I'm lucky. I'm the luckiest man in the world."

If you can't smile, borrow someone else's.

One time during my years as a baseball player, I'd just been sent back to Triple A ball, and my dad came to visit me in Montreal on a day when I was pitching so badly the manager took me out of the game. I was furious.

We went back to the hotel and ordered room service, and I was still complaining and alibiing until Dad had heard enough. "Keep your mouth shut," he told me. "I'm tired of hearing you complaining. I just came up here from Norristown [Pennsylvania] where it was so hot and humid it was hard to breathe, and here you are in an air-conditioned room, getting ready to eat steak, and you just called your wife long distance to say hello.

"She's healthy, you're healthy and working at a job you love. So if you can't smile, borrow one from me!"

Of course, there are times when the Dodgers are losing and I don't feel like smiling, and in the dugout there's not a smile I can borrow—like when the Yankees beat us in the '77 World Series and again in the '78 World Series. I wasn't smiling when I said, "Dear Lord, if you can ever see it in your heart to put me in another World Series as a manager, please let it be against the Yankees."

And, as all Dodger fans will remember, in 1981 we played 'em again and we won. I wish my dad had been around. The smile I wore then was available to everybody!

Fathers, provoke not your children to anger, lest they be discouraged.

Colossians 3:21

I WILL ENCOURAGE YOU
Ben Kingsley

A few months ago I was invited to speak to a group of students who had seen me play the title role in the movie *Gandhi*. I accepted with pleasure—to be among the young is for me always invigorating and rejuvenating. One of the questions they asked was how I decided on my career. I remember the circumstances very clearly—and my father's reaction when I announced my plans.

You see, until the age of nineteen I studied science, intending to become a doctor like my father. The summer after I graduated from high school, on a very warm afternoon, I bought a "standing" ticket to see Shakespeare's *Richard III* at Stratford-Upon-Avon (a ticket to sit down was too expensive). Richard III is a brilliant, hunchbacked man driven by a deadly ambition. The actor cast in this demanding role was Ian Holm.

I stood riveted in back of the theater. As the crippled Richard III hitched forward and backward across the stage, explaining to the audience how one day he would be king, I too began limping back and forth to keep a minimum distance between me and this extraordinary performance, and eventually there were two Richard III's in the theater.

Halfway through Holm's mesmerizing performance I fainted out of excitement and the summer heat. I was taken outside and given a glass of water, and then I returned to the play and watched its horrible, bloody, murderous conclusion.

My parents were waiting for me at the end of the afternoon—with the news that I had an appointment for an interview at a medical school in three weeks. I remember standing upon the steps of the theater and telling them—somewhat pompously and quite confidently, as we do when we're nineteen—"This is where I want to be. This is what I want to do."

My father, a very philosophical man, looked at me thoughtfully. "All right," he said. "I will encourage you."

I will encourage you. **Is there a more valuable human gift than making that promise?**

From that time on, my craft has been slowly developing. And I have my father to thank for recognizing—and honoring—the extraordinary passion and enthusiasm that had been awakened in me. His encouragement was the enabling power that allowed me to begin my career-journey—and that has sustained me during the long years it takes to learn a craft.

I will encourage you. Is there a more valuable human gift than making that promise to a beginner—of any age?

I think not.

A LETTER TO MY FATHER ON MOTHER'S DAY

Carmen Ezelle

*D*ear Daddy,

My roommates are peering over my shoulder and trying to figure out why I'm sending you this Mother's Day card. They don't understand why a father rates recognition on a day that's usually reserved for honoring the female leader of a household. But I understand, Daddy.

When I was ten and Mama died, our relatives warned you that I "wouldn't turn out right" unless I was entrusted to the special care of a woman. They urged you either to remarry or allow me to be cared for by an aunt. During all their fussing, you took me and brother Marcus aside and asked us to help you make an important decision. Could the three of us still be a family now that Mama was with God? If we worked very hard, you said, we could do it. Marcus, who was then only twelve, put his arm around me and said we should try. I nodded, too. So, instead of allowing well-meaning relatives to take charge, you set about making our shattered household a home again.

Because Mama was always a stickler for good nutrition, you continued to see that Marcus and I were well-fed. Before assuming your duties as our county's tax collector each morning, you'd arise before dawn to dash around the kitchen, fix breakfast, and pack our lunches. Our meals were never assembly-line productions. During the winter, we were treated to pancakes and hot chocolate; other times we had eggs, ham, and toast. And for lunch we always had to tackle one of your special triple-decker sandwiches and a thermos full of home-made chili.

Our suppers were also painstakingly prepared. Often, you would take time from your lunch hour to come home, set the table, and get a head start on dinner. There's nothing like coming home from school to the warming smells of supper in the making, and you made sure that we didn't miss that special pleasure. The three of us would then put the final touches on the meal. And before digging in, we would pray because, as you used to say, as long as we were feeding our bodies, we had to nurture our souls.

And, Daddy, you remembered the small, silly things that are important in any home. Every week you would bring home flowers for the livingroom vase. And remember the morning I casually remarked how I missed Mama's chocolate cake? When I got home from school that day, I found you in the kitchen, surrounded by mixing bowls and chocolate squares; and with a proud grin, you pointed to a freshly baked chocolate cake.

You and Mama had a dream about your children going to college, and you held us to that dream. Marcus was a great student, but I confess that I was a lazy one. Any other father—who had worked a long day and completed chores to boot—might have let a stubborn daughter do as she pleased. But I'm glad that you didn't give in to me. When it came time for choosing a college, you spent more time than I in the library, poring over college catalogues. "You've got to find a school that's just right," you insisted.

At that point, I guess I was more interested in finding a gown for my senior prom. All the girls at school had been planning their outfits with their mothers and I felt left out, cheated. Who was going to help *me*? Then, a few weekends before the prom, you announced over breakfast that the family was going shopping. And you took us into town to pick out my "special" dress. I must have tried on at least fifty gowns and exasperated an equal number of salesladies. Finally I stepped into a blue velvet empire gown, embroidered with tiny flowers. When I walked out of the dressing room, both you and Marcus stared intently, and then showered me with your approval. You *ohhed* and *ahhed* and told me I looked beautiful—and I *felt* beautiful.

Then it was time for me to begin college, and the day that you drove me to the dorm was a hectic one. You had a midday appointment back at the office, and we both rushed to carry the bags to my new room. As you sped off to work, I realized that you had gone without kissing me goodbye. "Never mind," I said to myself, and went to find some lunch in the dorm cafeteria. It must have been an hour later when someone motioned for me to look by the door. There you were, doing your best to catch my attention, yet remain inconspicuous. You were clear across town when you remembered my "good-luck" kiss. Appointment or no appointment, you explained, nothing meant more to you than wishing me luck. So with everyone watching, we stood there laughing, crying, and hugging each other.

That loving act was symbolic of your whole life, Daddy. Even when it took away from your personal time, you thought of your children. For you, kids' chatter was just as important as a Sunday-afternoon football game. And helping with arithmetic homework was often more important than bowling with the fellas on Thursday nights. Maybe, I admit, you weren't Superdad all the time, but you did work small miracles, and you showed your children love in some very special ways.

More than anyone else I know, you deserve to be remembered today.

Happy Mother's Day, Daddy.

Love,
Carmen

When I was a boy of fourteen, my father was so ignorant I could hardly stand to have the old man around. But when I got to be twenty-one, I was astonished at how much he had learned in seven years.

Mark Twain

YOU GAVE ME CONFIDENCE
Sue Monk Kidd

*I*t's Father's Day, Daddy, and here I sit wrapping your gift, filled with memories about growing up as your daughter. For instance, do you remember that time long ago when I went on my first dinner date? I was pretty young and shy, and still liked horses better than boys. But you encouraged me to go out. You knew I'd have a fine time.

A corsage came that afternoon. I will never forget the way my heart turned over when I lifted it out of the box. You said I must be very special to get flowers. Me—special? I couldn't stop looking at them. I studied myself in the mirror, wishing I were prettier. I had an awful scratch on my nose. But when it was time for me to go, you said I looked beautiful. Those were your very words.

"Don't stay out too late," Mama said, laughing. You smiled too, and tapped your watch. I was so nervous I slammed the car door on the hem of my dress.

At the restaurant I was sure everybody was staring at me. Hadn't they ever seen two people on a date? Or was it my nose everyone was gazing at? I felt awkward—you know how unsure of myself I was in those days.

The table was just for two with a candle glowing on it. Conversation was easier than I'd expected. Now that I think about it, it was I who did all the talking.

I kept talking right through dessert, about how I wished I could grow up to be a nurse or a writer and travel to Africa to take care of starving children. I was full of dreams back then. They seemed pretty unlikely to me, but that night I talked about them, and somehow started to believe I could do some of those things.

Then when I came back home, I was kissed on the cheek. I wanted to say in return, "Thanks for the corsage and the dinner and for making an uncertain girl feel so special." But none of that came out. All I could say to my date was, "You're too much!" I said it over and over. In the language of a twelve-year-old that meant someone was too wonderful for words.

You can be anything you want to be. Just believe in yourself.

Well, Daddy, I'm almost finished wrapping your gift now. But suddenly it doesn't seem like very much. A shirt. Did I give you a shirt last year too? Why do my gifts at Father's Day always seem so inadequate? Is it because I know deep inside that no matter what I give, you have given me still more?

You gave me confidence in myself twenty-five years ago. How was it you put it? "You can be anything you want to be. Just believe in yourself." That's what you said the night we dined in that restaurant on our one and only "date." And even today, when words don't come, I still say, "You're too much, Daddy!" You really are.

IN HIS HAND
Irene McDermott

*I*n his hand—how safe I have felt there since I was five years old. We lived in the country then, and I attended first grade in a one-room schoolhouse a mile from our farm. One morning in early fall I walked to school beneath a threatening sky. I hoped it wouldn't rain; I'd outgrown my raincoat and boots.

Just before school let out, though, the clouds let loose. My classmates took their slickers from hooks on the wall, stepped into their boots, and marched into the rain as happily as ducks waddling into a pond.

Only Miss Miller, my teacher, and I were left, and she was working at her desk, unaware that I was there. I had been in school only a few weeks, and I was too shy to tell this formidable teacher that I was afraid to walk home alone through the rain.

But at last I made for the door, slipping silently past Miss Miller. I stood at the threshold, listening to the hard rain splattering on the stone steps, trying to steel myself to leave. Oh, the fear I had. And then I heard another sound and . . .

Looking up, I saw my father. He was smiling at me. His hat was on the back of his head. He held a big black umbrella in one hand, and with the the other he swept me up and hugged me. And then we walked home along the country road, my hand tucked in his, the rain tapping on our umbrella.

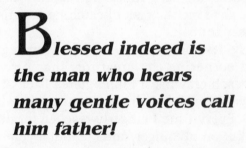

Blessed indeed is
the man who hears
many gentle voices call
him father!

Lydia Maria Child

A Good Catch

Daniel Schantz

*O*n a summer day when I was twelve, my father and I went fishing for bass in a small stream deep in the woods. He gave me the task of catching crawfish, whose tails we used for bait.

That day, I waded in the shallows, turning over flat rocks and cornering the creatures that lurked in the mud. But each crawfish I found glared back at me with beady eyes, waving his sharp pinchers, warning me to stay away. Every time I gingerly reached for one, a claw snapped shut on my finger, and I let out a yelp.

Finally my father came to my rescue and showed me how to do it. With one swift motion he grabbed a crawfish in his hand.

"You have to grab him firmly," Dad explained. "Play with him and he'll get you every time."

Time and again I've remembered Dad's advice, for as it worked with crawfish, I've found it's worked for me in confronting life's problems. "Deal courageously," Dad said to me later that day, quoting from the Bible, "and the LORD shall be with the good" (II Chronicles 19:11).

As usual, Father knew best.

DAD AND HIS HOMESPUN PHILOSOPHY
Tennessee Ernie Ford

*W*hen I was a kid our family had a rough time finan-
cially. As they say down in Bristol, Tennessee, where I
grew up, we just "never seemed to get a horn that
blowed."

Dad was in the postal service. He started out with a
rural horse and buggy route, then graduated to town and
walked his route for seventeen years, most of which
were pretty lean.

Yet we kids never thought of ourselves as poor,
because my dad had a faith so geared to appreciation and
joy that we thought we were pretty near on top of the
world. If he couldn't give us *things*, he gave us what was
a sight better, practical lessons in how to live.

First off he'd tell us: "Learn to look around you; see
and appreciate the bounty of God." He was talking
about the world God made without any help from us.
Ever since, I've always figured that an atheist was someone who'd never been deer huntin,' or blackberryin' or
pea pickin'. Because there's a terrific lot of beauty
around and a lot else to appreciate that's for free . . .
things we couldn't make and that we had nothing to do
with putting there. Seeing this beauty and the free gifts
of the earth and sky put joy in our hearts—and then we
had to share that too.

One of Dad's favorite illustrations was to remind us
of the fact that we had liberty and the guys down in the
town jail didn't. Also, that we had a lot of free music in

us, pretty good music, too, because we practiced both at home and in the church choir. Then on frequent occasions we would all go down to the jail, Dad, us boys, Mother, too, and we'd stand in the hall and sing—folk songs, ballads, hymns—a lot of hymns—because Dad thought they were the best for cheering people up.

At other times we would load up our old car with baskets of things from our own garden and our neighbors' gardens, plus fruit and stuff my mother had canned, plus game we'd bagged out hunting. Then we'd drive to the edge of town where the less fortunate people lived. After we unloaded our baskets, we'd sing for them.

Learn to look around you; see and appreciate the bounty of God.

One man, who had been in the jail on one of our hymn singing nights, came 'round to see Dad when he got out. He allowed as how he was a vagrant, a bum, a petty thief, and a drinking man when he could afford it. But he'd been attracted by the robust good cheer of our hymns. "That I liked," he admitted, "but this regular religion stuff cramps your style. It keeps you from having any fun!"

"Don't you believe it," roared my dad. He was six-feet-two, slender, and his enthusiasm for living had a way of vibrating in his voice. When it did, he seemed eight feet tall.

"Why, man, God has given us all these things to enjoy! We're *supposed* to enjoy 'em. You go over-doin' things, though, and you're bound to get sick, or a hang-over. But you use a little of the common sense God gave you, along with his other gifts, and you won't wear a long face. Religion is a real happy thing!"

It sure was a load off that guy's mind. And he proved it was true, too, because he settled down in our town to work, and he joined the church. He had a lot of fun, too.

Dad never tried to make us "good" through fear. "You'll have to be good through love, or 'twont go more'n skin deep," he said.

Our church life was really happy too. We prayed and sang and listened to Bible readings and sermons with great fervor. And then we had socials, dances, 'possum hunts, hay rides, and we did all this with great fervor, too. I came by hymn singing just naturally, the same way I came by my faith. I grew up with it. My folks made it a part of everything we did every day, and that made it personal and practical as well as natural.

I married my wife, Betty, during World War II when I was a bombardier in the Air Force. When the war was over we were back in Bristol, and me with no job in sight. We decided to try California, still with no job. It wasn't easy for a while, but neither of us lost faith in God. Nor did I lose faith in myself. I seemed to have a voice, a talent, but I had to appreciate where the talent came from, to be grateful for it, to share it—and that's the way it worked out.

Betty and I have two sons now: Jeff, eight, and Brian, five.* Life moves so fast these days that it takes some doing to get the boys out where they see God's bounty natural-like, instead of processed and packaged at the super-market. But it's got to be that way every so often

*Written in 1959.

if they're to get that direct, personal feeling about it. So we have a place at Clear Lake where there's lots of fish, and a ranch nearby where we raise cattle and watch things grow.

Not so long ago Brian gave good evidence that he's getting that personal feeling. He was received, in a baptismal ceremony, into the First Methodist Church of North Hollywood, our present church home. The whole event impressed him, including the certificate he received giving date, church name, minister, and other particulars. Reporting it later he said: "I didn't cry. I stood up there real good. The minister put water on my head and, oh . . ." suddenly his face lit up and he produced his certificate. "Look, I got a letter from Jesus."

So far I haven't been able to lure my dad to Hollywood; his roots in Tennessee go too deep. He's retired now after thirty-nine years in the postal service, and he has even more time to hunt and fish.

He isn't much interested in the money I'm making, or how many of the guest stars on my television show I call by their first name. But he wants to know, have I been to the lake? How is the farm?

What he's really asking is, has "gettin' me a horn that blowed" made me forget what I learned from him back there in Tennessee?

And I can honestly answer, no. For what he taught me has made it all possible.

CHOOSE ONE CHAIR
Luciano Pavarotti

*W*hen I was a boy, my father was a baker and my mother worked in a cigar factory. My father introduced me to the wonders of song. Our house was filled with recordings of the great tenors—Caruso, Gigli, Pertile, Schipa, Bjoerling, Tucker, all of them. When I was growing up, either the record player in our apartment was going full blast or Father and I were singing. He had a fine tenor voice; still has. He was the church soloist and sang in all music productions in Modena, our hometown, a small city in Italy's Po Valley. In Modena, everybody sang. We had our own opera house. Imagine! A 1,200-seat opera house in a town of 100,000 people.

Mother loved my singing. "Your voice touches me whenever you sing," she'd say. But she thought I should become an athletic instructor because I was so good at soccer—or at least an accountant.

My father urged me to develop my voice. "But you will have to study very hard, Luciano," he said. "Practice harder, and then maybe . . ."

If you try to sit on two chairs, you will fall between them. For life, you must choose one chair.

I sang two songs for Arrigo Pola, a teacher and professional tenor in Modena. He agreed to teach me without fees because he found some qualities in my voice which he thought should be developed. I also enrolled in a teachers college. On graduating I again asked my father, "Shall I be a teacher or a singer?"

"Luciano," my father said, "if you try to sit on two chairs, you will fall between them. For life, you must choose one chair."

I chose one. It took seven years of study, hard work, frustration, and rejection before I made my first professional appearance. It took another seven to reach the Metropolitan Opera.

I was blessed with a good voice by God. I think it pleased him that I decided to devote myself to it. And now I think whether it's laying bricks, driving a straight nail, writing a book, whatever we choose we should give ourselves to it. Commitment, that's the key. *Choose one chair.*

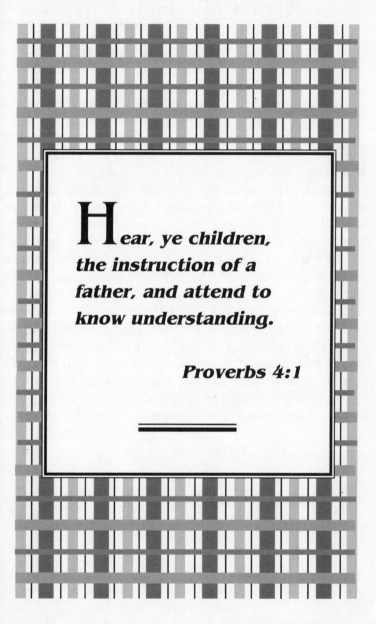

Hear, ye children, the instruction of a father, and attend to know understanding.

Proverbs 4:1

ALL I NEEDED TO KNOW
Charles J. Gordon

*W*hen I was growing up, my dad and I loved to challenge each other with puzzles and brainteasers. When we watched TV, he'd quiz me on details, such as the make of a cowboy's rifle or the model of a policeman's car. One of his favorite tests was to stump me by moving one thing in a room—a picture, a chair, the salt or pepper shaker—and then ask, "What's different in this room?"

Each day he and I walked the same route home, though at different times, and at supper we would question each other about things we saw. One evening he said, "I hid a penny along the way home. Can you tell me what date was on it?" For four days I looked, finally finding it in plain sight. Though these tests of our powers of observation were just games, they brought us close.

He put all I needed to know where I'd always be able to find it . . .

I grew up, and my parents moved away. Shortly before Dad died at the age of fifty-two, he made a visit to see me. One afternoon while on a walk to enjoy the fall foliage, we talked about the possibility of his death and the problems that might arise. There would be my parents' business and numerous other matters that I might not know how to handle.

Questions were tumbling out of me when Dad put his hand on my shoulder and said, "Jimmy, don't worry. The answers you'll need are in a place where you can find them."

After his funeral that conversation haunted me. Was this one of our games? Was there really a place where he had left me some answers? I began a search. I looked in his safe-deposit box and went carefully through his desk, then moved on to less obvious places, such as his coin collection and his toolboxes. To no avail. Meanwhile business decisions had to be made with Mom. I did what I thought was right, always praying that it *was* right, but still I had nagging doubts. Where were those answers Dad had said I could find?

One day eight years after Dad's death, I overheard my son asking his older sister how she remembered to tie her shoelaces. She replied, "I've got it written down inside my heart so I won't forget, ever."

I stood looking at her in amazement. She understood something I'd overlooked since Dad's death. Long ago, through our games and tests, Dad had been teaching me how to look at life carefully. By learning from him I'd become the man, father, and husband I was. He put all I needed to know where I'd always be able to find it—in my heart.

GETTING TO KNOW DAD

Larry DiBiaso

*I*t wasn't until I was in college that I realized I didn't know my father.

Not that I didn't have one. Dad was always there—a stocky, rugged man who was about the best carpenter in Georgetown, Massachusetts. He was always kept busy around our little town, so busy that when I was a youngster, we never really seemed to get to know each other. Besides, he was a quiet man who didn't find talking very easy.

I can remember his getting home late in the evening, warming his big gnarled hands around a mug of hot coffee, and sitting quietly. I'd try to tell him about my Little League or the football team I had made, and he'd nod and listen. But Dad wasn't really interested in those things.

But he did know I loved to fish. And though he never fished himself, he took the time one winter to build me a small rowboat. Almost every evening that summer, after delivering my papers, I could be found out in the boat on the town pond with my dog perched in the bow while I matched wits with a few wise old trout.

I guess it really hit me one fall afternoon years later, as I sat in my dorm at Northeastern University in Boston, reading a letter from Mom. She mentioned that my old rowboat had finally fallen victim to the elements. I sat there a long time looking out the window into the wizened empty trees and thinking of my dad—

how he built that little boat; how he worked so hard to build other people's homes in order to make ours secure.

"Dad, oh Dad," I sighed within, longing for a companionship we never had. I smiled, remembering when, while building the boat, he tried to initiate me into the secrets of his profession. But I seemingly never inherited any of his talent.

Had there been anything we had in common other than our heritage? And then, like that last ray of sun on a dark winter's evening, a sudden thought intrigued me.

During those winter nights in our workshop, as we built the boat, there was one thing that had brought us together, something through which Dad tried to please me, but knew nothing much of himself: fishing.

My opportunity came during winter vacation. After the holiday festivities were over, I said, "Dad, how about going ice fishing, just the two of us? I know a pond in New Hampshire where they're waiting in line to get our bait."

> **. . . Our lives suddenly flowed together in that intimate relationship all fathers and sons should share.**

Thus it was early one icy morning which found us walking out on the shadowy silver ice of Sandown Pond. The sun was still only a rose blush through the black lace of the pines which crowded the shore. It was so still that one could hear the dull muttering of the ice beneath us. Steam rose from our nostrils as we walked along in that silent communication of shared adventure.

Then I showed Dad how to chip out the fishing holes so that we had four of them, each about eight inches in diameter. I took out the tip-ups, arranging each one over its slushy hole with the wriggling shiner bait down in the black water. At the first nibble, the small red flag would pop up.

As the sun, now a fluorescent orange, climbed above the pines, the pungent smoke of our fire warmed our ice-pinched nostrils.

Suddenly Dad scrambled across the ice.

A red flag was up!

Grabbing the line he pulled up a flapping silver pickerel. "Wahoo!" he whooped in exultation, holding the pickerel as if it were a diamond brooch.

From then on he watched those tip-ups like a birddog eyeing pheasants.

But something else happened out on that pond: a melting of an elusive barrier so that our lives suddenly flowed together in that intimate relationship all fathers and sons should share.

Like the thawing of an ice-bound brook, our conversation began to melt free, first in rivulets and then in an easy flow.

I learned about my family's heritage, how my grandfather came over from Italy as a teenager, first to labor on the railroad and then to realize his American dream with his own small grocery store. I learned how Dad always prized being able to work outside, and I was surprised to find he had always had an interest in all outdoor things.

We found we had so much to talk about that we almost forgot the tip-ups. But not quite.

When the sun reached the pines on the other side of the pond, we had thirty perch and twenty pickerel.

Reluctantly we climbed into the old pickup truck, then sat there for a moment watching the sun's afterglow bloom above us. "That was great," Dad said quietly.

After I returned to school, Dad went right on fishing. And many times I'd be with him, having discovered that Boston wasn't that far away from home. Afterward Mom would write that "he gets so much fun out of it. The only thing is," she added half grudgingly, "I've had to learn twenty-five new ways to cook fish."

Dad celebrated his new interest to me through letters filled with descriptions of other ponds discovered and snapshots of record catches.

He and Mom still live in Georgetown. I'm married and now take my own son fishing.

Last spring Mom phoned. Dad had been helping raise a big beam and had ruptured three discs in his back.

He was in terrible pain. The doctors recommended surgery. But Dad, always a stubborn man, would have none of it. I drove up there, and we discussed it all one evening—talking was easy now. Finally he was convinced that the doctors knew best.

Mom and I waited outside the operating room and prayed. After four long hours the doctor emerged to say that the surgery was a success. The next morning the nurses ushered us into Dad's room.

He heard my step and turned his head. "Hi, Son," he said, smiling. His work-scarred hand grabbed mine. His eyes were luminous. In them I could see the sun rising above Sandown Pond one frosty morning.

DAD FINDS A BUDDY
B. David Edens

*R*aymond Camp, who authored the column "Wood, Fish and Stream" for *The New York Times*, once received a letter from a boy. It read, "Would you tell me where I could find a place to fish that is not more than five or six miles from my home in Queens? I am fourteen years old and have saved up enough money to buy a rod, reel, and line, but do not know where to go fishing. My father goes almost every weekend, but he fishes with older men who do not want a boy along, so I have to find some place I can reach on my bicycle or the subway."

By resorting to the telephone directory, the columnist was able to obtain the father's name and sent him his son's letter with a brief note. He received this reply from the father, "You handed me quite a wallop in your letter, but I am sorry you did not hit me harder and sooner. When I think of the opportunity I might have lost, it frightens me. I do not need to point out that I now have a new fishing companion, and we have already planned a busy spring and summer. I wonder how many other fathers are passing up similar opportunities?"

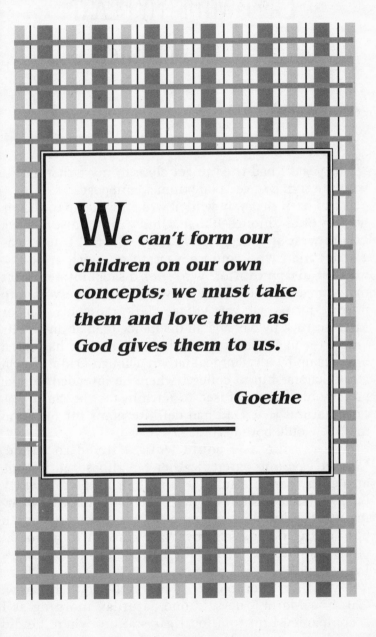

We can't form our children on our own concepts; we must take them and love them as God gives them to us.

Goethe

DEEP WITHIN MY HEART
Carol Lawrence

*F*or years I had tried to get close to my father, but it was like trying to get a hug from a lamppost.

It had been that way while I was growing up too. Ours was an old-fashioned Italian family in Melrose Park, a suburb west of Chicago. My father, Michael Laraia, was a strict man who could devastate me with a look, a word of disapproval or, worse, of disappointment. Yet my younger brother and I knew he worked very hard to provide for us. He was village clerk and controller for Melrose Park by day and an insurance man at night. His ambition had been to be a lawyer, but he had been brought up by a tyrannical father. Though Dad had won a full scholarship to college, where he intended to take prelaw, his father refused to let him take it. So it was only natural that Dad had definite plans for Joey and me: We would both become lawyers.

Yet as soon as I could walk, I loved to dance. Mother gave me patent leather tap shoes and lessons at a local dance studio. From then on I constantly tapped all those shuffles, flaps, and ball changes, wearing out the kitchen linoleum. By age thirteen I began performing during summer vacations in local social clubs and later danced in the ballet corps of Chicago's Lyric Opera.

My father tolerated it. "That is all right for now, Carolina Maria," he said one Saturday morning as I accompanied him to a local gas station, where he did the owner's accounting. "But I will be so proud when I can point you out in a courtroom and say, 'That is my *figlia.*' "

I smiled and looked out the window. These Saturday mornings with Dad were so precious that I did not want to break the spell.

When I graduated from Proviso High School with a scholarship to Northwestern University, he was ecstatic. He expected me to take prelaw. Instead, I was named freshman of the year in drama.

The following summer on a family vacation to New York, I found a spot in a Broadway chorus line. My mother was delighted; my father was crestfallen. He hardly said a word to me. After I found a room, they immediately left for home.

In 1957 I got my big break, singing the lead role of Maria in *West Side Story* on Broadway. From then on life was a whirl of musicals, television specials, and dramas.

In the meantime my brother, Joey, became a successful lawyer. I married Robert Goulet. Two sons came along. And even though it seemed my father had finally accepted my career, conversations with him were stiff and formal.

Even during the heartbreak years, when my marriage crumbled and I struggled alone to raise my boys, working harder than ever to make ends meet, Father and I remained coolly polite. It was Mother who heard my anguished cries. Yet even she could not fill that empty space within me. More and more I felt that God had stopped loving me because I had not done everything right. I desperately sought some kind of forgiveness, some kind of relief from the guilt that burdened me.

Though I had drifted away from God through the years,

I was suddenly drawn to a local church. There I found a warmth and spontaneity I had never known before. Instead of warning me about God's displeasure, the pastor talked about God's unconditional love and reminded us that Jesus told us to love thy neighbor *as thyself*. And I began to understand I couldn't love anybody in a healthy way until I learned to love and accept myself. I joined a women's prayer group, where I could unload my guilt in confidence without fear of being judged.

Knowing finally that God had forgiven me with all my faults, I began to look outward. And I experienced the unexpected joy of devoting time and effort to understanding others. One morning I was inspired to do something I had never considered before.

As I waited at a gas station, the pungent odor of gasoline triggered memories, and once again I was sitting at my father's side in that Melrose Park gas station long ago. A warmth filled me, and I thought of all those unfortunate people I knew who, estranged from a friend or relative, awaited the other person's gesture of reconciliation. So often it came too late. And I remembered a pastor's telling me that when Jesus asked us to forgive others seven times seventy, he meant we should swallow our pride and take the first step. I knew what I must do.

That night I wrote Dad a long letter. Into it I poured all the love of a skinny little girl. I told him how I'd idolized him and followed him around like a puppy because he epitomized patience, wisdom, understanding, and uncompromising truth.

"Dad, you always had the answer I needed," I wrote, "or knew how to mend whatever I had broken." I told how I marveled at his struggle from the poverty of immigrant status to the success of a highly respected official and businessman.

"Dad, I'm proud to be your daughter," I wrote, "and everybody else, including Mom and Joey, knows how much I really love you. I just wanted you to know it too." I mailed it that night with a profound sense of relief at having done something I should have done long ago.

Later I booked a concert just outside of Chicago for one special reason: Mother had phoned that Dad's health had become critical. He had been living with cancer for some years, but now it was devastating him. The concert would be the second part of my letter. I prayed he'd be well enough to attend.

When I called home to let my parents know when I would arrive, I asked Mother if I could talk to Dad. He got on the phone.

"Dad, did you get my note?"

"Yes," he said, "thank you for a lovely letter."

A lovely letter? Couldn't he at least. . . ? But no, I couldn't let such a thought deter me from reaching for reconciliation. I had no right to expect an emotional outpouring.

While waiting in the auditorium the night of the concert, I was terribly nervous. I had front-row seats set up with special cushions for Dad. Would he be there? I felt like I was six years old and performing for the very first time. Then I saw him coming, with Mom and Joey. His frail frame was bent slightly forward, his thin white hair shining in the auditorium lights. They sat down in front of me.

The comedy numbers were easy, but when I sang ballads, I had to watch the catch in my throat. The most difficult was the close. I was to blow a final kiss to the audience.

"This has been a special time I'll always cherish and

keep deep within my heart," I told the people, "and so until next we meet, please remember that"—the orchestra began to play—"you will be my music."

My father looked into my eyes and nodded his head approvingly.

"You will be my song."

He nodded again.

"You will be my music, to fill my heart with love my whole life long."

And then I saw Dad lift his glasses to brush away a tear, and I had to look away for a second. Then Joey helped my father to his feet, and Dad stood clapping and smiling, tears streaming down his face. As I watched him, I was thankful I had taken that first step toward reconciliation. I threw him a kiss and felt my heart whole.

Finally, after Dad died, I learned how complete that reconciliation was. My sister-in-law told me, "You'll never know how much your letter meant to your father. He was so proud of it and would read it to us over and over again. In truth, he had it memorized." Then she added, "We found your letter in your father's pajamas shirt pocket where he always kept it, right over his heart."

I bowed my head. Just where I had always wanted to be.

An angry father is
most cruel toward him-
self.

Publilius Syrus
Moral Sayings

Prodigal Father
Dale Kugler, Jr.

At seventy-three, Marcia Pollock's father was a man of great independence, a man of great pride. He had been an ironworker, a career that gave him great satisfaction, even looking back. He loved to point out to his grandchildren the construction jobs he had worked on, the huge advertising structures in Times Square, some of New York's mightiest bridges. The kids called him "Poppy," a contagious name that everybody used.

Poppy lived in a furnished room in his old neighborhood, and he had a job, part-time, at Baltz's Pharmacy. After Marcia's mother died, Poppy had firmly and flatly refused Marcia and Jack's invitation to come live with them. He was stubborn about not intruding on their lives, about not crowding their little house, about not becoming a burden.

Yet the truth of the matter was that they really wanted him. Poppy was good to be around. He was always on the up side, always helpful. The kids loved him because he listened to them and worked with them and because, too, he always brought them something. There were always special gifts on birthdays and at Christmas. And whether it was a little bunch of bachelor buttons for Marcia or a new after-shave from Baltz's for Jack, Poppy simply never arrived empty-handed.

And so it was with shock and bewilderment that Marcia went to see Poppy in the hospital that summer. He had collapsed in the street. The doctors told Marcia Poppy had been living on coffee and doughnuts.

"Why, Poppy, why?" Marcia wanted to know. "There's no reason to go without food. You have money. You have us. . . ." But Poppy just brushed the whole subject aside.

"You're wrong," Otto Baltz told Marcia later that day. "He has practically no money at all—just the government check and what little he makes here. Yet I myself saw him spend most of his last check on your little boy's bicycle."

She became stern with Poppy. "You're foolish, Poppy," she said.

"I have my pride," Poppy answered.

"False pride," she hurled back at him.

During autumn, Poppy didn't come around as often as he had in the past, but when he did, he would still arrive with little gifts in hand, and he would look at Marcia with a defiance she had never seen in him.

"I can't come over Christmas Day," Poppy told her just before the holidays. "This year I promised I'd watch the store."

Marcia knew Baltz's was not open on Christmas.

From then on she grew more distressed with each day that passed. She had to do something, but she floundered until the morning she sat down and wrote the letter.

Poppy dear—
This will be brief. We'll miss you at Christmas, all of us, because you are one of us. I am praying for you—as always.

And, Poppy, lately I've been thinking about the parable of the prodigal son and its meaning for Christians, especially in the confusion of Christmas. What's more important in that situation, the destruction of pride—or the triumph of love?

We love you.
Marcia

All Christmas morning Marcia thought about Poppy.

Half an hour before the turkey went on the table, the doorbell rang. Marcia jumped. She knew it was Poppy.

The kids rushed to him and in their great surprise inundated Poppy with more hugs and kisses than he had ever had before. Poppy then looked at Marcia. Now there was no defiance in his eyes, only snap and sparkle like the Poppy of old. Yet there was something else, a look of triumph, the look of a battle won.

Poppy held out his arms to Marcia, and his hands, those strong ironworker's hands, were empty, utterly empty—yet never had they been more filled.

On returning home after being away for a week I swept up our two-year-old as he ran to me, arms out-stretched, calling, "Daddy! Daddy!" My heart soared as I lifted him and hugged him. . . . And then I thought that this must be how our heavenly Father feels when we turn to him and tell him how much we love him.

Alistair Hamilton

Children are an heritage of the Lord: the fruit of the womb is his reward. As arrows are in the hand of a mighty man; so are children of the youth. Happy is the man that hath his quiver full of them.

Psalm 127:3-5a

THIS IS MY DADDY
John D. Garwood

*I*f I live to be a hundred years old, Son, I will never forget yesterday—that hazy, mellow, October day. It was the day you and your little first grade friends had chosen to visit our college campus.

The students from my last class were hurriedly leaving. Do you remember, Son, as I was gathering up my papers how you stood in the doorway, cap in hand, and said, "Hi, Daddy!"

"Now what do you want?" I asked impatiently.

You smiled that big smile of yours and said that you wanted me to come with you to see the campus, and look for red leaves . . .

Was that an unreasonable request? I guess I thought so. I was busy. I had lectures to prepare, papers to grade, a meeting to attend.

You had stepped in some mud . . . you had filled your pockets with leaves—I scolded you for that.

Through it all you remained silent, Son, with kind of a hurt look on your face as I paraded these things before you.

After I finished you said, in a small voice, "Will you come, Daddy?"

"Can't you see I don't have time?" I said. Your nose wrinkled; your eyes squeezed shut.

"All right, stop crying. I'll come for a little while."

You clung tightly to my hand as we joined your friends. And then things happened.

"This is my daddy," you said to Tommy. "This is the fellow I've been telling you about." You wanted all your friends to see me.

It hit me then, Son. Your little heart was running over with affection and love for me. You were more than willing to overlook my angry words and lack of appreciation for you, but I had to make you cry before I could find time to spend with my boy.

> **How could any father who sees the love and trust in the eyes of his [child] doubt the existence of a God?**

Standing there, Son, with your hand in mine, I remembered all the times I had robbed myself of the privilege of sharing your joys and your griefs. Soon it will be too late for me to do this.

Standing there under the golden trees in that autumn haze, I had a glimpse of how lucky I am. How could any father who sees the love and trust in the eyes of his son doubt the existence of a God, and the love and benevolence of that Deity?

As the years roll by, when your mother and I sit at home waiting for the postman to deliver your letters, I'll think back, Son, to that October afternoon when the leaves were falling . . . when you took me by the hand and proudly told your companions, "This is my daddy."

WALK A LITTLE PLAINER, DADDY

"Walk a little plainer, Daddy," said a little child
  so small.
"I'm following in your footsteps, and I don't
  want to fall.
Sometimes your steps are very plain,
Sometimes they're hard to see;
so walk a little plainer, Daddy, you are leading
  me.
I know that once you walked this way
many years ago, and what you did along the
  way,
I'd really like to know.
For sometimes when I'm tempted, I don't know
  what to do;
so walk a little plainer, Daddy, for I must follow you.
Someday when I'm grown up, you are like I
  want to be;
then I will have a little child who will want to
  follow me.
I would want to lead just right knowing I was
  true;
so walk a little plainer, Daddy,

I MUST FOLLOW YOU."

Anonymous

DEAR DAD
"Elaine"

*Y*ou may think you've never done much for me, since you scarcely saw us after you and mom were separated when I was eight. But I want you to know that I made a very important discovery through you, and I thank you for it.

I had never been able to accept the idea that God could love me because I was so full of failings and sins and I didn't deserve love. Oh, I could understand why he might love me in my moments of goodness and beauty and generosity—but all of the time?

And then, without your even knowing it, you helped me understand God's kind of love.

Grandma had died, and a little bit of my life went with her. You came into town for the funeral, and you sat in front of me at the service. I tried to think of Grandma during the eulogies, but I think she guided my thoughts to you.

I could only see the back of your head and the curve of your jaw. Your hair was still thick and the gray that blended in and showed over your ears was, as all things seem to be on you, handsome. Your neck was tan and lined from the sun and somehow vulnerable looking. The light shown on the tip of your mustache when you turned your head. Your shoulders seemed smaller than I remembered—fathers are so big in their children's minds.

Suddenly in a rush of feeling I didn't even expect, I

was overwhelmed with love for you. A really warm, vital, living love for a father who was a literal stranger to me, whom I had seen only every few years and for only a few minutes at those times, for a father who hadn't wanted me, for a father whose memory held more unpleasantness than good. It surprised me and it made me cry. I thought the tears were for Grandma, but they weren't, Dad—they were for you, and me.

So you see, I love you. I don't love you because you deserve it; you don't have to deserve it. I don't love you because you're a kind, thoughtful, unselfish, lovable father; you probably aren't. I love you because I love you. You don't have to love me in return, although I think you do deep inside. You don't even have to want my love—you've got it. But it would make me happier if you accepted it and said so. And that's all God asks of us.

Now, finally, I have learned about God's love. Thank you, Dad.

Love,
Elaine

MORE TO BEING A FATHER
Dick Van Patten

I felt a small tug at my shirtsleeve.

"Dadd-*eee!*" The exasperated tone in my son's voice told me it was probably his third or fourth attempt to get attention. Seated at the dining-room table of our home in Bellrose Village, Long Island, I'd been absorbed in theater trade papers, desperately searching for an acting job. It was summer, 1963, and I hadn't worked for three months.

"What is it?" I asked irritably.

"Daddy," he said, hopefully, "let's go play catch, okay?"

Nels was eight, blond, blue-eyed, the eldest of our three sons. Suddenly, from out of nowhere, his brothers appeared.

"Yeah, Daddy," said seven-year-old Jimmy, "let's go out and play!"

"Come on, Daddy," piped six-year-old Vincent. "*Please!*"

"Daddy's busy," I heard my wife Pat say, shepherding the kids toward the kitchen.

I returned to the papers, but couldn't concentrate. My work had always meant everything to me. *Everything.* Besides, my idea of being a good husband and father was based upon being a good provider. I felt like a failure.

I stood up and walked over to the living-room window. With sadness, I recalled how happy Pat and I had been when we moved here as a young couple six years ago. When I met Pat, she had her own successful career as a professional dancer; she'd given it all up to marry me and raise our family.

Back then I was still riding high on the wave of success following my long-running role as Nels on the popular *I Remember Mama* TV series, sure I'd go on to be a star. After all, I'd been acting since childhood.

I still recalled vividly my first audition. I was seven years old. My grandmother accompanied me to the neighborhood theater in Queens, where MGM Studios was sponsoring a child personality contest. Grandma Van Patten had lived with us for as long as I could remember. I guess at that time she was just about my best friend. Now she remained by my side until I was called before the judges to recite my poem. "You can do it," she whispered, squeezing my shoulder reassuringly.

When I won the contest, which resulted in a four-month contract, Grandma was the one who moved with me to Hollywood. I was fifteen when she died. By then, I'd acted in numerous Broadway shows and was working and studying under Alfred Lunt and Lynn Fontanne. I was always glad that Grandma had lived to see my success. *But,* I thought ruefully, *good thing she isn't around to see me now . . .*

In recent years, I'd found myself having to accept smaller and smaller parts. There was no good explanation why, and I didn't know what to do about it. Not even in church could I find comfort or guidance. My own prayers seemed flat, vague. As I grew increasingly irritable and impatient, my behavior was taking its toll on my family—especially my sons.

I felt the gentle touch of my wife's hand on my shoulder. "Dick," she said softly, "don't worry."

I gave her the same annoyed look I had earlier given

my son. But Pat's concerned expression remained unchanged. "Honey," she said, "I think maybe we should pray about this."

"Pray? Don't you think I do?"

"I mean," she said quietly, "let's pray together. Let's pray specifically. You know you've always said you've never prayed without receiving an answer."

Pat was right. I did have faith in a personal God, and strong belief in the power of prayer. But this problem of a declining career and no money coming in was so big—I didn't know how to pray about it.

Pat seemed to sense my thoughts.

"God knows what's best for us," she said. "Let's simply ask him to get us through this summer according to his will." She paused. "Okay?"

"Yes," I said dully. "Okay."

Holding hands, we stood by the window and prayed.

I didn't feel any better.

A few more weeks passed. Nothing changed. Pat asked if I would mind if she tried auditioning for some local dance productions. I wasn't crazy about the idea. But, reluctantly, I agreed. We needed the money.

One muggy morning, I was seated at the dining-room table, scanning the trade papers, when Pat rushed in, breathless and smiling. She had just auditioned for a summer production of *Hit the Deck*, at Jones Beach.

"Guess what!" she gasped. "I got the job! They want me in the chorus! And the pay's not bad!"

Instead of being pleased, I felt my stomach tighten into a knot.

"That's great," I said tersely. "That's real nice, Pat."

She came over and hugged me. "Rehearsals begin tomorrow," she said. "I'll be gone a lot during the days. You'll be all right taking care of the kids, won't you?"

"Yeah," I said. "Fine."

"Don't you see?" Pat continued. "This is the answer to our prayer."

It was an answer, all right, but it sure wasn't the one I'd been hoping for.

When Pat was working, I didn't really mind taking care of the kids. That is, I didn't mind the duties involved.

What bothered me was the way God had chosen to answer our prayers. True, thanks to Pat's income, we were "getting through the summer." But what long-term good could ever come from this situation? It sure wasn't helping my career.

One hot afternoon as I was putting away the last of the lunch dishes, Jimmy entered the kitchen.

"Daddy, can we go to Greenwood?"

"Greenwood" was Brooklyn's Greenwood Cemetery, where my grandmother was buried. The kids loved visiting Greenwood; with six square miles of wooded grounds, four lakes, lots of wildlife and great shady trees to climb, it was more like a park. Only twenty minutes away, it was, for our family, a place of good times and happy memories. *Why not?* I thought. *We haven't been to Greenwood in ages.*

"That's not a bad idea," I said. "Get your brothers, and let's go."

Once at Greenwood, we walked the familiar hilly path to Great-grandma Van Patten's grave. We talked a little about what a wise, loving lady Great-grandma had been, about how happy she must be up in heaven and watching us down here on earth. As we talked, I felt myself relaxing, forgetting the tensions of unemployment.

Then we sat cross-legged on the soft green grass and

121

decided what game we'd play. "How about looking for the oldest marker?" I suggested.

"Yeah!" The boys agreed. The game was a family favorite.

"Remember the rules?" I asked.

Big brother Nels was quick to remind us. "Ten minutes to search; report back here when we hear Daddy whistle; then we see who wins."

"That's right," I said, and we set boundaries for our area of play.

"Ready?" I asked. Three heads nodded. "On your mark—Get set—Go!"

A mad scramble, and we were off—running and stopping, peering and bobbing, as we hunted for epitaphs of long ago. Caught up in the game, I felt like a kid myself. Before I knew it, I was daydreaming about my own childhood—and about Grandma Van Patten. She was always there . . . her steady blue eyes shining, her voice encouraging, her gentle touch conveying her trust and love for a little boy.

> **For the first time, I fully appreciated that, next to God, my *family* had to be the most important thing in my life.**

I found a tall, leafy tree and leaned against its massive trunk. In the distance, I heard the whoops and hollers of my kids having a good time.

I shut my eyes, allowing my thoughts to drift . . .

Why, I wondered, *had Grandma spent so many hours with me? Surely she must have had better things to do. But she'd always been so selfless, so generous with her time—as though being with me was genuinely important to her. Our times together had meant so much to me. I'd been so self-absorbed lately—so wrapped up in worry about my career. Perhaps*—I felt a twinge of guilt at the idea—*perhaps there was more to being a good father than simply being a good provider. Could it be that God was trying to tell me that my sons might need and benefit from the same kind of love and attention that Grandma had given me?*

"Daddy!"

I opened my eyes to see my three sons standing over me with puzzled expressions.

"Daddy, we've been waiting for your whistle!"

"Daddy, it's been over ten minutes!"

"Daddy," said Vincent, accusingly, "you've been *sleeping*!"

"Come on, you guys," I said gruffly, "I was just resting. Now, who found the oldest marker?"

> **Even in this rapidly changing world, the family *can* work . . . it remains God's will for his children. It's up to us to live in accordance with that plan.**

But in the minutes that had passed, something had happened to me. Surrounded by my happily chattering boys,

I felt my heart melting. How precious my sons were ... how short was our time together ... how much I loved them! For the first time, I fully appreciated that, next to God, my *family* had to be the most important thing in my life—even more important than my career. And with that realization, a great imbalance was corrected in my heart. The weight of worry about getting work had lifted; God, I knew, would take care of that in his own time.

I was also beginning to understand a little better how God works. By keeping me home for the summer, he had shown me how to appreciate and love my family in a new way that otherwise would have been impossible. This was a lesson worth more than all the jobs in the world. It was the kind of lesson—I smiled to myself— that Grandma Van Patten would be pleased to know I'd learned.

After that sunny afternoon in Greenwood, I considered each day an opportunity to grow closer to my family. The rock-solid foundation of love and trust that was established proved to be invaluable later. In 1970, we moved to Hollywood, where the stresses and strains of show-biz careers have been known to destroy the strongest ties.

Today, we remain as close as ever.

Thousands of years ago it was written, "And he will turn the hearts of fathers to their children and the hearts of children to their fathers" (Malachi 4:6 RSV). I'm convinced that even in this rapidly changing world, the family *can* work—that it remains God's will for his children. It's up to us to live in accordance with that plan.

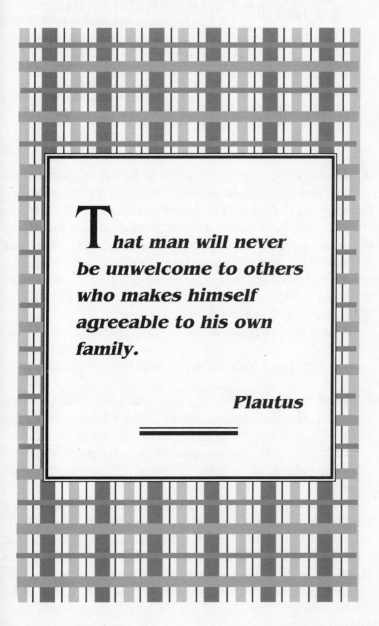

That man will never
be unwelcome to others
who makes himself
agreeable to his own
family.

Plautus

How can I make myself want to be a good father?

Charlie W. Shedd

*H*ow can I make myself *want* to be a good father?"

As a newspaper columnist, I get this question in my mailbox all the time. The letter writer says, "To be perfectly frank, I get so carried away with making it big in the business world, my family winds up way down on my agenda. I know I should spend more time with my children. I also know my wife deserves more attention than she's getting from me. But how can I make myself *want* it the way it should be?"

I have three suggestions:

1. We can admit we aren't what we should be.

When we have faced that fact, we can reprogram our minds in the direction of home. Those demands of the office, the factory, shop, store, farm, business, profession are important. Yet, through all these externals, it is possible to keep a clear internal focus on the family. But here again comes the question, "How?"

A salesman friend of mine spends many hours in his car. Every week he drives off to earn a living for his family. But if you could see the sun visors in his car, you'd smile. Drawings from his six-year-old; notes from his third-grade daughter; a picture of his son in a baseball uniform; some special mementos from his wife; all of these keeping his soul programmed back to his home and family.

That's his way, and we all can work out our own way if we really try.

2. Agree to specific time commitments—some compacts from Dad to his wife, to his children, and all of them together.

"Listen, troops, from now on every Saturday night is family night. Get your other stuff out of the way, no exceptions. Saturday night is for all of us. We'll go to dinner, go for a ride, go somewhere together. Or maybe we'll do something special at home if that's what we decide to do. Anything so we can be together."

Maybe you think that kind of an announcement is a bit thin in democracy. But do you know any children, any wife who wouldn't be glad to hear it? Most family time these days won't happen unless we make it sacrosanct, and keep it that way.

Another dad told me, "We have five kids, and every week I take one of them out alone. Breakfast, lunch, dinner. Out with me eyeball to eyeball. I also do the same thing with my wife. When you know you're going to spend time with them and they know it too, you look forward to it, and they do. Then you really can talk over things. So you ask how a man finds time for his family? Well, he doesn't find time; he has to make it."

3. One more suggestion: A long look down the road may be a help today.

When our family is raised, when we're older and our children are all grown up, how will we feel then about what we're concentrating on right now?

Sure our children may disappoint us. No guarantee

that they won't. They may not think at all like we think. Their life-style could be a shocker. But way down there in the future when we're old and can't do much but recollect, it would be great if we could say, "I may not have been the greatest parent or husband, but I gave it all I had."

There was a famous football coach who resigned. "It's great," the coach said: "No tension with players, no worries with management. No ulcers from 'Will we make it to the Superbowl?' "

But one thing kept bugging him. "All those years I was coaching, I worried about my family. How were they doing, not being with them enough. Believe me, I've been looking forward to making up for some lost time. Well, take it from me, that whole bit is overrated. Way overrated. The kids are off doing their own thing; this one here, that one there. My wife, too—she has a life of her own. Sometimes I hardly see her either. So here I am, sitting home, watching the soap operas."

Sorry about that, Coach. But some things simply won't wait. And it's so easy to rationalize: "Someday off in the future, I'll have more time. Then I'll be the right kind of dad, the attentive husband, the better family man. Or will I? Will my family even be there for togetherness?"

He waited too long. The time to get started in being a family is right now.